Program Authors

Peter Afflerbach

Camille Blachowicz

Candy Dawson Boyd

Wendy Cheyney

Connie Juel

Edward Kame'enui

Donald Leu

Jeanne Paratore

P. David Pearson

Sam Sebesta

Deborah Simmons

Sharon Vaughn

Susan Watts-Taffe

Karen Kring Wixson

Editorial Offices: Glenview, Illinois • Parsippany, New Jersey • New York, New York
Sales Offices: Needham, Massachusetts • Duluth, Georgia • Glenview, Illinois
Coppell, Texas • Sacramento, California • Mesa, Arizona

About the Cover Artist

When Scott Gustafson was in grade school, he spent most of his spare time drawing pictures. Now he gets to make pictures for a living. Before he starts a painting, he photographs his family, pets, or friends posing as characters that will appear in the illustration. He then uses the photos to inspire the finished picture. In this cover you can see his pet cockatiel, Piper.

ISBN: 0-328-10834-0

10 11 12 13 14 V063 14 13 12 11 10

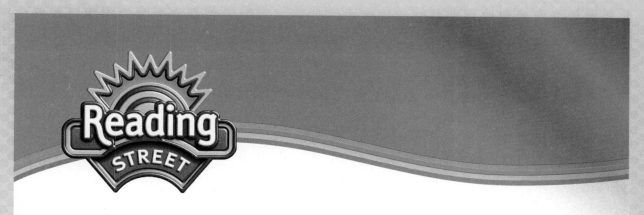

Dear Reader,

    Has your trip down *Scott Foresman Reading Street*
been exciting so far? We hope so. Are you ready for more?
In this book you will find out about pumpkins and frogs and
what happens one dark night. You will read about baseball,
cowboys, our country's flag, and a boy who gets into trouble
making signs. Each time you turn a corner, you will learn
something new. But you will also have many chances to use
what you learned before. We hope you'll have fun doing it.

    Sit back and enjoy the trip!

            Sincerely,
            The Authors

OUR CHANGING WORLD

Read It
ONLINE
sfsuccessnet.com

How do things change?
How do they stay the same?

Responsibility

What does it mean to be responsible?

Read It
ONLINE
sfsuccessnet.com

Traditions

How are traditions and celebrations important to our lives?

Read It
ONLINE
sfsuccessnet.com

OUR CHANGING WORLD

How do things change?
How do they stay the same?

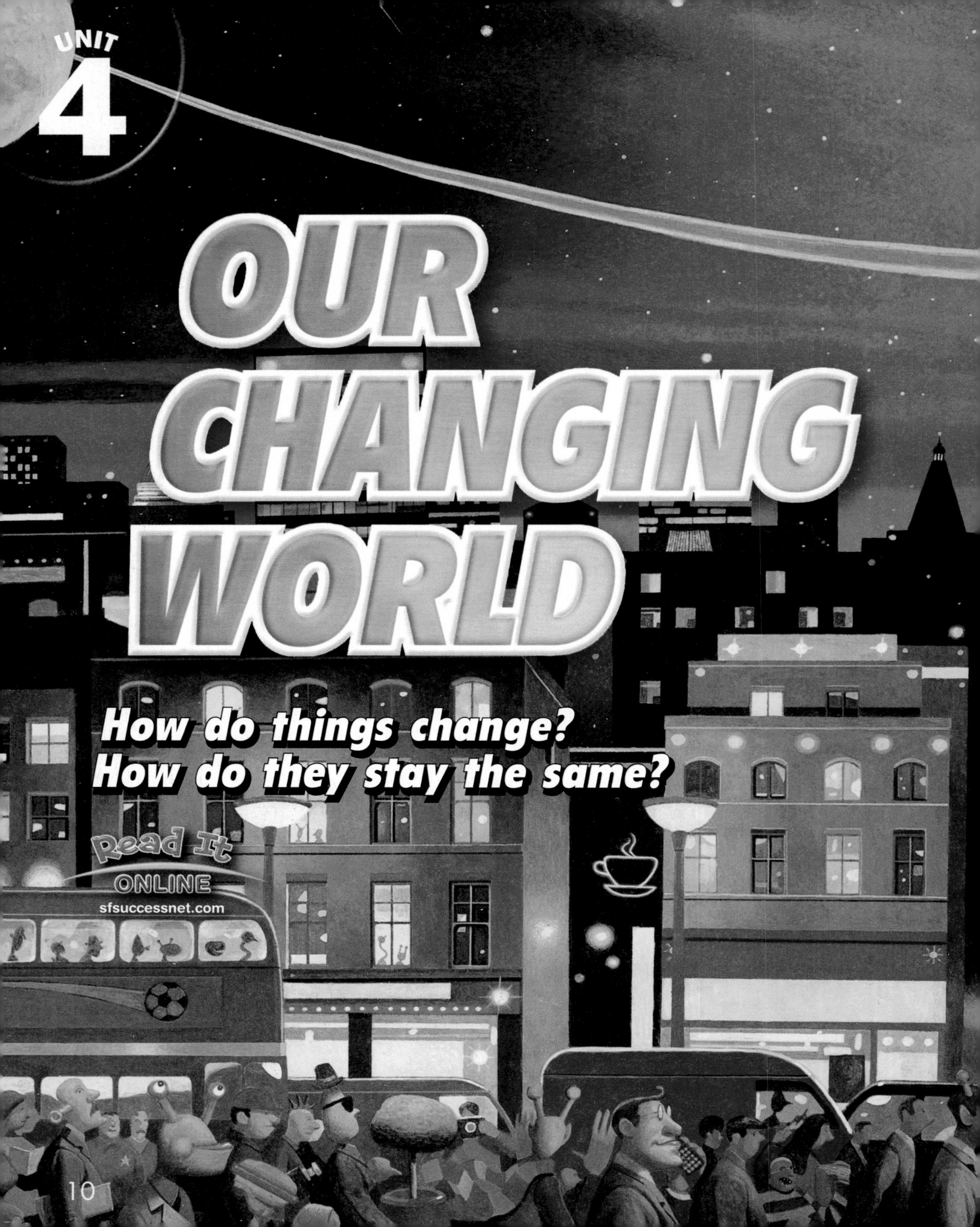

Read It
ONLINE
sfsuccessnet.com

Skill

Compare and Contrast

- When you compare and contrast, you see how things are alike and different.

- Words such as *like, also, but,* and *unlike* are clues that something is being compared.

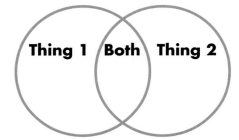

Thing 1 Both Thing 2

Strategy

Strategy: Story Structure

Active readers notice what happens at the beginning, middle, and end of a story. You can compare a character's feelings or actions at different parts of the story.

1. Read "Cookie Bakers." Fill in a diagram like the one above to show how the two cookies are alike and different.

2. Use your diagram to write a sentence that tells how the cookies are alike. Then write a sentence telling how they are different.

Cookie Bakers

Darrell thought his mother made the best cookies. She mixed oatmeal and peanut butter. She rolled big balls of dough. When the cookies were done, she let Darrell taste the first one. It was warm and delicious.

One day Darrell said, "Mom, look what I found in this old box!"

"Those are Grandma's recipes," his mother said. She looked through the old yellow bits of paper. Then she stopped at one. "Cookies! Let's make some of Grandma's cookies!"

"But your cookies are best," Darrell said.

His mother went ahead. She read Grandma's recipe. First, she took out some oatmeal, but she did not add peanut butter. Instead, she added chocolate chips. Unlike her usual big balls of dough, she made small ones. At last the cookies were done.

"Have the first one," she told Darrell. Darrell ate it. It was warm and delicious.

Strategy
At the beginning of the story we find out how Darrell feels about Mom's cookies. Let's find out what happens in the middle.

Skill Some clue words in this paragraph tell how the two cookies are different—*but* and *unlike*. How are they alike?

13

blankets

quilt

stuffing

wrapped

trunks

unpacked

pretended

Remember

Try the strategy. Then, if you need more help, use your glossary or a dictionary.

Vocabulary Strategy

for Prefixes

Word Structure Sometimes as you read, you may come across a word you don't know. Look at the word. Does it have a prefix at the beginning? When the prefix *un-* is added to a word, it makes the word mean "the opposite of _____ ." For example, *untied* means the opposite of *tied.* You may be able to use the prefix *un-* to help you figure out the meaning of the word.

1. Put your finger over the prefix.

2. Look at the base word. Put the base word in the phrase "the opposite of _____ ."

3. Try your meaning in the sentence. Does it make sense?

Read "Going West." Look for words that begin with *un-*. Use the prefix to help you figure out the meanings of the words.

Going West

In 1844 the Wilsons headed west to Oregon. They traveled in a covered wagon pulled by two oxen. In the wagon was everything they needed for the trip. They also had everything they needed to begin their new life in Oregon.

Friends told the Wilsons to bring lots of blankets and quilts. A quilt is a cover for a bed. To make a quilt, Mrs. Wilson put cotton or wool between two pieces of cloth. Then she sewed the pieces of cloth together. This stuffing made the quilt thick and soft.

Mrs. Wilson used all of her quilts. She wrapped her dishes in some quilts. Then she packed the quilts into trunks. The trunks would not be unpacked for four months. The Wilsons used some quilts as beds. They folded quilts and put them on the wagon seats. The quilts made the hard seats softer. They unfolded other quilts and hung them inside the wagon to keep out the wind and the dust. Jimmy Wilson even wrapped a quilt around himself and pretended it was a cape!

Write

Make a list of five things that you think the Wilsons should have in their wagon. Use words from the Words to Know list.

The Quilt Story

by Tony Johnston
illustrated by Tomie dePaola

Genre **Realistic fiction** tells about events that could happen in real life. Read about what happens to a little girl's quilt.

How does a quilt change as time passes?

A little girl's mother
made the quilt
to keep her warm
when the snow came down,
long ago.

She stitched a quilt
by a yellow flame,
humming all the time.
She stitched a tail of
falling stars.
And she stitched the name,
Abigail.

Abigail loved the quilt.
She wrapped it round her
in the quiet dark
and watched the winter skies.
Sometimes she saw a falling star.

Sometimes Abigail
played in the woods
near her home.
She had tea.
Her dolls had tea.
And the quilt had tea
all over it.

Sometimes she pretended
the quilt was a gown.
She wore it to town
on her horse,
clop, clop, clop.
And it tore.

So her mother
stitched it up
once more.

Sometimes she played
hide-and-seek
with her sisters.
She laughed and cried,
"Don't peek!"
and hid under the quilt.
And everyone found her.

Sometimes Abigail
was sick.
She sneezed
and sneezed.
Then she slept
under the quilt.
And she felt better.

One day Abigail's family
moved away, across wide rivers
and over a rock-hard trail.

The quilt went too.
Not stuffed in trunks
with the blankets
and clothes. It kept
the little girls warm
from the wild winds.
Warm from the rain.
Warm from the
sparkling nights.

They built a new house
in the woods.
Abigail's father built it
with his hatchet,
chop, chop, chop.
He built her a new bed,
chip, chip, chip.

He made her
a new horse too.
He worked until
curly shavings
covered the floor
and everyone sneezed
and said, "Welcome
home," and was glad.
And Abigail felt sad.

New house.
New horse.
New bed.
Everything smelled of
fresh chops and chips.
Everything but the quilt.

So her mother rocked
her as mothers do.
Then tucked her in.
And Abigail felt
at home again
under the quilt.

One day when the quilt
was very old and very loved,
Abigail folded it carefully
and put it in the attic.
Everyone forgot it
was there.

A grey mouse came
and loved the quilt.
Her babies were born
on top of it.
They grew fat and grey
in the warm stuffing.
When they got hungry,
they ate a falling star.

A raccoon came and loved
the quilt. She dug a hole
in a corner with her
black paws and hid
an apple there.

A cat came
and loved the quilt.
A patchwork cat.
It rolled on the stars,
and stuffing spilled
out like snow. Then
the cat curled up in
the snow and purred.

"Kitty, Kitty,"
called a little girl.
She found her cat
and she found the
quilt, splashed with
patterns of sun.

The little girl wrapped
the quilt round her.
And she loved it too.

27

"Can you make it like new?" she asked her mother.

So her mother patched the holes. She pushed fresh stuffing in. She stitched long tails on the stars to swish across the quilt again.

One day the little girl's family moved away,
across miles and miles of pavement
and snaking grey highways.

They found a new house.
Freshly cleaned.
Freshly waxed.
Freshly painted. White.

They unpacked and
unpacked. All night.
And everyone sneezed
on cardboard dust
and said, "Welcome
home," and was glad.
And the little girl
felt sad.

Everything smelled of
white paint and boxes.
Everything but the
quilt. So her mother
rocked her as mothers
do. Then tucked her in.
And she felt at home
again under the quilt.

Reader Response

Open for Discussion What story would you tell if you were Abigail's quilt?

1. This story doesn't happen in one day. How does the author show that the story happens over a long time?

2. How did Abigail and the second little girl feel about the quilt? Compare and contrast their feelings.

3. *The Quilt Story* is told over time. Name an event that happens before Abigail moves and another that happens after she moves.

4. Make a web. Put the word *quilt* in the center. Add words that tell how the quilt was used.

Look Back and Write Look back at pages 25 and 26. Three animals visited the quilt in the attic. Who were they and what did they do with the quilt? Use details from the selection in your answer.

Read more books by Tony Johnston.

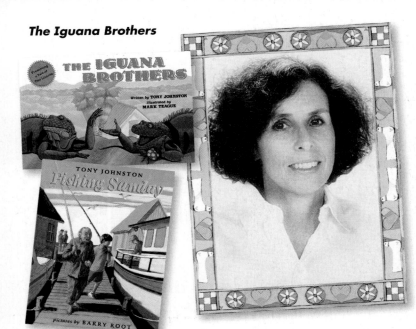

The Iguana Brothers

Fishing Sunday

When Tony Johnston was young, she wanted to be a veterinarian or a "bugologist." She collected everything that flew or crawled. She even raised monarch butterflies. But when Tony grew up she became a teacher, and she sometimes wrote stories for her students. Another teacher saw her talent and encouraged her to become a writer. Ms. Johnston says, "As soon as I realized how hard (and satisfying) it was, I was hooked."

She has gone on to write more than 80 children's books. She and her family have lived in New York, Mexico, and California.

32

Tomie dePaola

Read more books written and illustrated by Tomie dePaola.

Tomie dePaola says that his goals as a child were to write stories, draw pictures for books, and to sing and tap dance on the stage. He has now done all these things.

Mr. dePaola uses his own childhood for ideas too. His Italian grandmother was the model for the grandmother in *Watch Out for the Chicken Feet in Your Soup*. He has written or illustrated over 200 books and won many awards for them. He lives in New Hampshire with his two dogs, Moffat and Markus.

Adelita: A Mexican Cinderella Story

Things Will Never Be the Same

Interview

Genre

- An interview records a conversation between two people about a specific topic.

- One person asks questions, while the other person answers them.

Text Features

- The text of an interview uses a question-and-answer format.

- Abbreviations in dark print tell who is talking.

- Photos often help explain the topic.

Link to Social Studies

Design a quilt to commemorate your community. Brainstorm ideas with your classmates.

Making Memories
Changing with the Times

an interview with
Mary Jane McDonald

by Myka-Lynne Sokoloff

Mary Jane McDonald tells about a special quilt she helped make. It was made for the 200th birthday of Brewster, Massachusetts.

Myka-Lynne Sokoloff: In the past, quilts were very useful. They covered beds and kept people warm. What is different about this quilt?

Mary Jane McDonald: Old quilts were made from old clothing and bits of fabric people had around their houses. The idea of buying new fabric and tearing it up seems odd to some people. It's a changing art form.

We're a long way from the kinds of quilts that were made from old dresses, old tablecloths, and old linens to use up the last bits. The pioneers used everything they possibly could. They threw very little away.

MLS: Times have changed, haven't they?

MJM: We live in a throw-away society now.

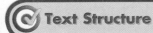 **Text Structure**   What do you notice about the format of this selection?

MLS: Tell me about the Brewster quilt. Who worked on that?

MJM: Anyone who lived in town could work on it.

MLS: How did you choose the pictures that would go on the quilt?

MJM: We wanted to make a map of Brewster. Then we placed the map on the background. We started with the sky, then the ocean, and then sand. After that, it started to grow like weeds.

MLS: How did you choose which buildings to put on the map?

MJM: We made a list. We decided that the church was important. It started in 1700. We felt the store was important. It was a meeting place in town. We wanted to include the old and the new.

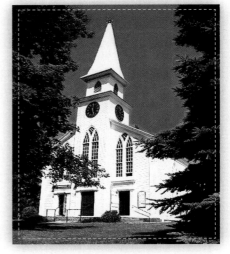

A church has been on this spot for 300 years.

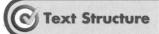
Text Structure How did the format help make your reading easier?

People still gather at The Brewster Store today.

Many sea captains lived in Brewster long ago. This sea captain's home is on the quilt.

MLS: You were trying to show how the town had changed?

MJM: Yes. We wanted to make it new but still show the important things from the past.

MLS: It seems like the quilt really did change over time. You really didn't have a design in mind. You didn't cut the pieces to fit a pattern. It just grew?

MJM: Yes, that's right. We decided we needed some old sea captains' houses, because this is a town of sea captains. We put in the bike path, which used to be the railroad track.

MLS: What do you hope people will learn when they look at the quilt?

MJM: Just a sense of Brewster— what it has to offer.

The quilt hangs in the town library. People may see it there 200 years from now. They will see how the town has changed.

Reading Across Texts

The quilts in *The Quilt Story* and in this interview were made for different reasons. What were the reasons?

Writing Across Texts

Make a chart that tells who made each quilt, why they made it, and who enjoyed it the most.

Compare and Contrast Compare Brewster today with Brewster 200 years ago.

Adjectives and Our Senses

An **adjective** describes a person, place, animal, or thing. An **adjective** can tell how something looks, sounds, tastes, feels, or smells.

One day Abigail's family moved away, across **wide** rivers.

Wide describes the way the rivers looked.

The new house smelled of **fresh** chops and chips.

Fresh describes how the chops and chips smelled.

Write Using Adjectives

1. Find a sentence in the story that uses an adjective to tell how something looks, sounds, or feels. Write the sentence. Underline the adjective.

· ·

2. Think about a blanket or quilt in your home. What does it look like or feel like? Write two sentences about the quilt or blanket. Use two or three adjectives in your sentences.

· ·

3. Abigail's family takes a long trip. What trip have you taken? Write three sentences about your trip. Use adjectives to describe your trip or what you saw.

Comprehension

Skill
Fact and Opinion

Strategy
Ask Questions

Skill

Fact and Opinion

- A statement of fact can be proved true or false. You can prove it by checking a book, asking someone who knows, or seeing for yourself.

- A statement of opinion tells someone's ideas or feelings. Clue words like *best, beautiful,* and *should* show statements of opinions.

Fact:	
Opinion:	

Strategy

Strategy: Ask Questions

Active readers ask themselves questions. As you read, ask yourself if a sentence is a fact or an opinion. Ask, "Can this sentence be proved true or false by checking it out?"

Write

1. Read "Our Red Oak." Make a chart like the one above. Write one statement of fact and one statement of opinion.

2. Read the statement of fact from your chart. Write at least two ways you could check whether it is true or false.

Our Red Oak

We have a great tree in our front yard. It is a tall red oak. My dad says it is 30 feet high. Our red oak is the best climbing tree.

Skill The word *best* in this sentence is a clue that this is an opinion.

The branches are thick and reach toward the ground. After I climb up in the tree, I hide behind the leaves. People down on the ground cannot even see me.

I like to look at the leaves too. They are quite beautiful. Each leaf is about as long as my hand. The top part of the leaf is shiny and dark green. The bottom side of the leaf is fuzzy and a brown-red color. In the fall the leaves turn orange.

I tell friends that they can always find my house. It's the one with the best tree in town!

Strategy What question could you ask yourself to test whether the last sentence is a fact or an opinion?

43

Words to Know

fruit

smooth

vine

soil

root

harvest

bumpy

Remember

Try the strategy. Then, if you need more help, use your glossary or a dictionary.

Vocabulary Strategy

for Homonyms

Context Clues Sometimes when you read, you might see a word you know but the meaning doesn't make sense in the sentence. The words around it might help. The word may be a homonym. Homonyms are words that are pronounced and spelled the same but have different meanings. For example, *fly* means "a kind of insect." *Fly* also means "to move through the air with wings."

1. If the meaning of a word you know doesn't make sense in the sentence, look at the words around it. The word may be a homonym.

2. Use the words around it to figure out another meaning.

3. Try the new meaning in the sentence. Does it make sense?

As you read "Great Grapes" look for words that may be homonyms. Use nearby words to figure out which meaning makes sense in the sentence.

Great Grapes

Grapes are a kind of fruit. They are small, round, and smooth. They grow on a vine. Grapes come in many different colors, such as green, red, white, black, and blue.

Grape farmers cut and save parts of the old vines. Then they plant the parts in the soil. The parts take root and become new vines. The farmers hang wires between poles. The vines cling to the poles and grow up and across the wires. Vines use long, thin shoots, called tendrils, to hold on as they climb. The vines do not grow grapes for several years. But once they start growing grapes, they can grow them every year for as long as 100 years!

Grape harvest happens in the summer or fall. Farmers cut the grapes from the vines. Grapes for eating are put in boxes and shipped to market. Some grapes are spread out on paper and left in the sun. Soon they dry into small, bumpy raisins.

Write

What is your favorite fruit? Describe it. Tell a little about how it grows. Use words from the Words to Know list.

Life Cycle of a Pumpkin

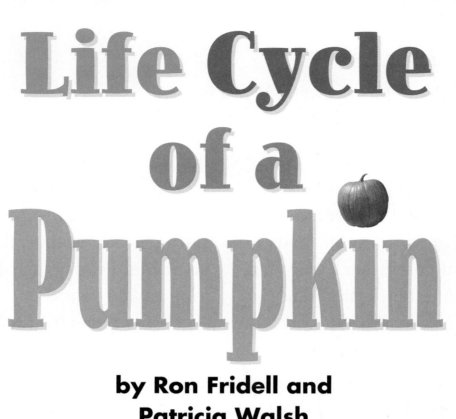

by Ron Fridell and Patricia Walsh

Genre

Expository nonfiction tells facts about a topic. Look for facts about how a pumpkin grows.

How does a pumpkin go from seed to pie?

What is a pumpkin?

A pumpkin is a fruit. It grows on a vine like other kinds of squash. Pumpkins can be bumpy or smooth, large or small, long or round. They can be orange, white, yellow, or red.

Each year there is a new crop of pumpkins. Their hard shells have deep lines that go from top to bottom.

Seed   1 week   2 weeks   10 weeks

Seed

Pumpkins begin as seeds. The seeds are white and have an oval shape. A tiny plant is curled up inside each seed.

The seed is planted in warm, moist soil. In about ten days, a root grows down into the soil. The root takes in water and food for the plant. Tiny leaves push up into the sunlight.

11 weeks

14 weeks

16 weeks

Seedling

The first two leaves pop through the soil. These are smooth seed leaves. They use sunlight and air to make food for the new plant.

Then the true leaves appear. They are jagged and prickly. The job of the seed leaves is done. They wither and fall off.

Seed

1 week

2 weeks

10 weeks

Vine

The pumpkin plant grows more leaves. The plant grows quickly and soon becomes a vine. The vine twists and creeps along the ground.

The vine sends out thin tendrils. They grab and curl around other vines. They twist around fences. The tendrils support the vine as it grows longer and longer.

11 weeks

14 weeks

16 weeks

Flower

The pumpkin vine blooms with many yellow flowers. Some of these are female flowers. Female flowers sit on small, fuzzy, green balls.

Other flowers are male flowers. They are on long stems and have yellow powder inside the flower. The yellow powder is pollen. It takes a male and a female flower to make a pumpkin.

Seed

1 week

2 weeks

10 weeks

Pollination

It also takes bees to make pumpkins. They move the pollen from male flowers to female flowers. When a bee visits the male flowers, the pollen sticks to the bee's body and legs.

The pollen rubs off the bee as it goes in and out of the flowers. When the pollen reaches a female flower, the fuzzy green ball at the end of the flower begins to grow into a pumpkin.

11 weeks

14 weeks

16 weeks

Growing and ripening

Late summer

All summer the vines, tendrils, and leaves of the plant grow and tangle together. Underneath the big leaves are little pumpkins.

The leaves are like big umbrellas. They keep the hot sun off the pumpkins. They also help to keep the soil around the pumpkins from drying out.

Seed

1 week

2 weeks

10 weeks

Problems for pumpkins

Growing pumpkins need just the right amount of water and sun. Too much rain rots the pumpkins. Too much sun withers the vines.

Cucumber beetles and squash bugs can hurt pumpkins too. Farmers spray the plant with insecticides or cover the vines with nets to protect the growing pumpkins.

11 weeks

14 weeks

16 weeks

Harvest

The pumpkins grow bigger and bigger. Inside, the pumpkins form seeds and pulp. Outside, the pumpkins turn from green to orange.

Then the vines turn brown. Harvest time has come. The farmer cuts the thick pumpkin stem from the vine.

Seed

1 week

2 weeks

10 weeks

56

After the harvest

Four months ago there were only seeds. Now the farmer has harvested a wagon full of round, orange pumpkins. They will be sold at farmstands and stores.

People cook pumpkins and use the pulp to make pumpkin pie, cookies, soup, and bread. Some pumpkins are fed to farm animals.

11 weeks

14 weeks

16 weeks

Festivals

Some towns hold a pumpkin festival to celebrate the fall harvest. Sometimes there is a contest to find out who grew the biggest pumpkin.

Inside the pumpkin are many seeds. Some seeds are roasted to be eaten as a snack. Other seeds are saved to be planted in the spring. They will grow into next year's pumpkins.

Seed

1 week

2 weeks

10 weeks

Next year's crop

After the pumpkins are picked and sold, the farmer plows the field. Old vines and unpicked pumpkins get mixed with the soil. The field is ready for planting seeds again next spring.

11 weeks

14 weeks

16 weeks

Reader Response

Open for Discussion What did you learn that you didn't know before? Talk about the most amazing or the most interesting thing you learned about pumpkins.

1. Look back at page 51. The author uses some interesting verbs, or action words. What words does the author use to show how hardworking the pumpkin vine is?

2. *Pumpkins grow on vines.*
Mom makes great pumpkin pies.
Which statement is a fact and which one is an opinion? How do you know?

3. What questions did you ask yourself as you read about pumpkins? What did you learn?

4. Make two columns. Label one *Noun* and the other *Adjective*. Under each, write words from the list and from the story that fit the category.

Look Back and Write What does it mean to say, "A bee is a friend of a pumpkin vine"? Look back at page 53. Use information from the selection to explain your answer.

Read more books by Ron Fridell and Patricia Walsh.

Ron Fridell and Patricia Walsh are married, and they are both writers. They often write their own books, but they wrote *Life Cycle of a Pumpkin* together.

Life Cycle of a Spider

Life Cycle of a Turtle

Mr. Fridell and Ms. Walsh do lots of research. They use the library and the Internet, but they like to see things themselves too. When they were doing research for this book, they went to a pumpkin festival not too far from their home in Illinois.

Mr. Fridell and Ms. Walsh love to travel. "We travel for adventure and the excitement of seeing new places. But we also travel to do research and get ideas for our books."

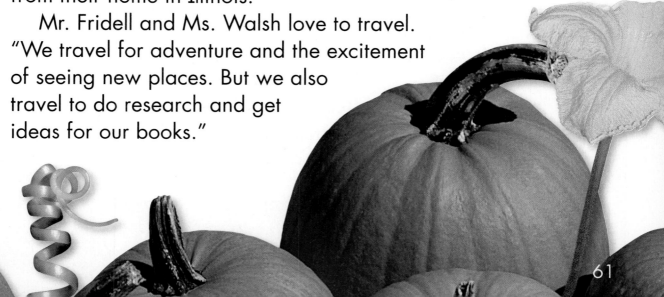

Genre

- Poems are often written with a certain rhythm. In this poem, almost every line has five syllables. This makes a clear rhythm.

- Many poems also rhyme, but not always. In this poem, the second line rhymes with the fourth line. This makes the poem fun to read.

Link to Writing

Try writing a poem about something in nature. Your poem might rhyme or it might not. If you wish, read your poem aloud for the class.

How do seeds know which way is UP?

by Amy Goldman Koss

It's dark underground
Where sunlight can't go,
So how does a seed
Know which way to grow?

The root is the first
To grow from the seed—
Down into the darkness
It digs at full speed.

Gravity sensors
Within each young root
Teach it to follow
A straight downward route.

And once this young root
Has taken the lead,
A tender green shoot
Sprouts out of the seed.

The shoot only knows
That its life's pursuit
Means heading the opposite
Way of the root.

Since shoots need the sunlight
To live and to grow,
They force themselves upward
Through dark dirt below.

The roots need the water
And the shoots need the light.
Each goes its own way,
And that works out just right!

Reading Across Texts

How is the plant in this poem like the pumpkin plant you read about in *Life Cycle of a Pumpkin?*

Writing Across Texts Draw a diagram of a seed sprouting into a plant. Label your diagram.

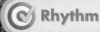 **Rhythm**   Clap each syllable to help you feel the rhythm of the poem.

Adjectives for Number, Size, and Shape

Words for number, size, and shape are **adjectives**. The words **a** and **an** are also adjectives.

In **ten** days, **a** root grows down into the soil.

Ten describes how many days. The word **a** describes how many roots—only one.

The seeds are white and have **oval** shapes.

Oval describes the shape of the seeds.

A **tiny** plant is curled up inside.

Tiny describes the size of the plant.

Write Using Adjectives for Number, Size, and Shape

1. Find a sentence in *Life Cycle of a Pumpkin* that uses an adjective to describe number, size, or shape. Write the sentence and underline the adjective.

- -

2. Think about fruits or vegetables you have grown or eaten. Write some sentences describing them. Use adjectives for number, size, and shape.

- -

3. Make a sign for selling pumpkins. The sign should make people want to buy pumpkins from you. Tell the size, shape, and number of pumpkins you are selling.

Comprehension

Skill
Compare
and Contrast

Strategy
Graphic
Organizers

Skill

Compare and Contrast

- When you compare and contrast things, you tell how they are alike and different.

- Clue words such as *both* and *like* show comparisons. Clue words such as *but* and *different* show contrasts.

Strategy

Strategy: Graphic Organizers

To help you compare and contrast things, make a chart. Write the items being compared at the top. Write *Alike* and *Different* at the tops of the columns.

Butterflies and Moths

Alike	Different

1. Read "What Is That Fluttering Insect?" Make a chart to compare the butterfly and the moth.

2. Use your chart. Write about how butterflies and moths are alike and how they are different.

What Is That Fluttering Insect?

A beautiful insect lands on a flower. Is it a butterfly or a moth?

Butterflies and moths look very much alike. Both have six legs and four wings. Both have feelers on their heads. But butterflies have round knobs at the end of their feelers. Moths' feelers are straight.

Butterflies and moths eat the same thing. They both drink nectar from flowers.

Butterflies and moths fly at different times. If you see such an insect during the day, it is likely a butterfly. If it is night, the insect is probably a moth.

Look also at how the insect holds its wings when resting. Most butterflies hold their wings straight up. Most moths rest with their wings spread flat out over their backs.

It can be hard to tell a butterfly from a moth. But look closely. You can do it!

Skill Here are some clue words. The words *alike* and *both* signal things that are the same. What does *but* signal?

Strategy Now, if you made a chart, you can add more information to it.

Moth

Butterfly

wonderful

shed

skin

crawls

insects

powerful

pond

Remember

Try the strategy. Then, if you need more help, use your glossary or a dictionary.

Vocabulary Strategy

for Suffixes

Word Structure When you read, you may come to a word you don't know. You might look for a suffix. Does the word have the suffix *-ful* at the end? The suffix *-ful* added to a word usually makes the word mean "full of ___." For example, *colorful* means "full of color." You may be able to use the suffix to help you figure out the meaning of the word.

1. Put your finger over the suffix *-ful*.

2. Look at the base word. Put the base word in the phrase "full of ___."

3. Try that meaning in the sentence. Does it make sense?

Read "Snakes." Look for words that end with *-ful*. Use the suffix to help you figure out the meanings of the words.

Snakes

Some people think snakes are scary. Others think they are wonderful animals. Snakes do not have legs. They slide across the ground on their bellies. Their eyes are always open. They have no eyelids. They can smell with their tongues. As a snake grows, it must shed its skin. A snake crawls out of its old skin and leaves it behind. Imagine if people did that!

Some snakes eat insects, such as ants. But most snakes eat fish, birds, frogs, and rats. They can swallow these animals whole because they have jaws that open very wide.

Some snakes use their powerful muscles to squeeze an animal until it stops breathing. Then the snake eats it.

Snakes live almost everywhere on Earth. Some live in water, such as a pond or an ocean. Others live in the desert or the forest. Some live underground, and some can even climb trees. You can see why some people think snakes are wonderful animals.

Write

Did the writer change your ideas about snakes? Write what you think about snakes. Use words from the Words to Know list.

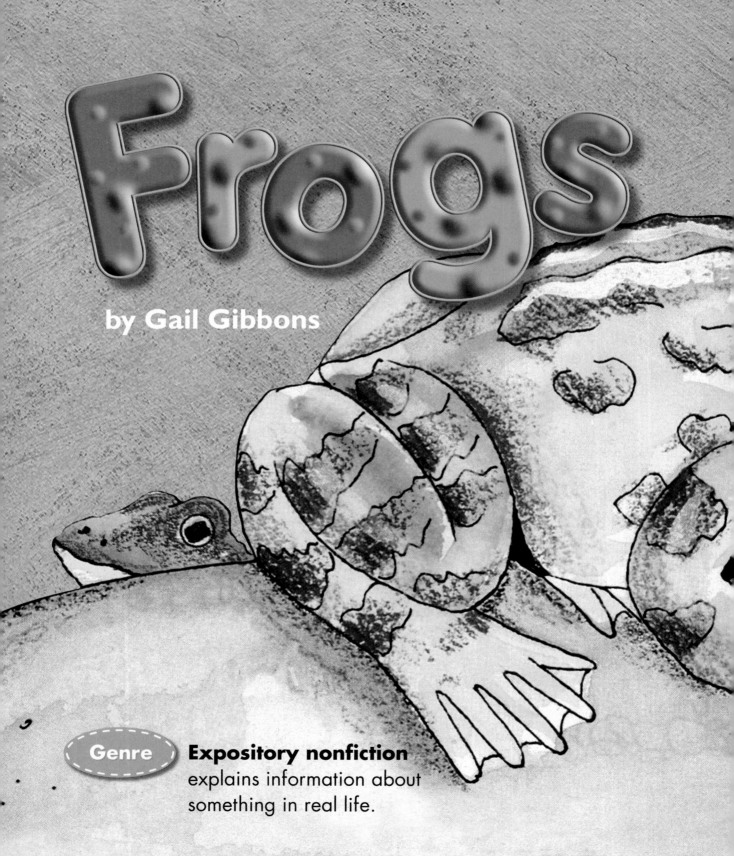

Frogs

by Gail Gibbons

70

What will you learn about frogs that you didn't know before?

71

Frog Spawn

It is springtime at a pond.

A jellylike cluster of eggs floats among the waterweeds at the pond's surface. These eggs are the beginning of . . . frogs.

A breeze ripples the surface. The floating clump of eggs is called frog spawn. Frogs lay their eggs in water or wet places. Otherwise, the eggs could dry up and die.

These eggs do not have shells. They are inside jellylike coverings. As they float, the jelly lets the sun's warmth come through to the eggs inside. Not all the eggs will survive.

Most of the time the large and slimy mass of eggs is too slippery and too big to be eaten. This is nature's way of protecting them. But some of the smaller clusters of eggs will be eaten by creatures living in or near the pond.

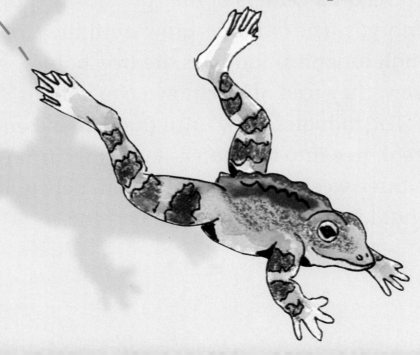

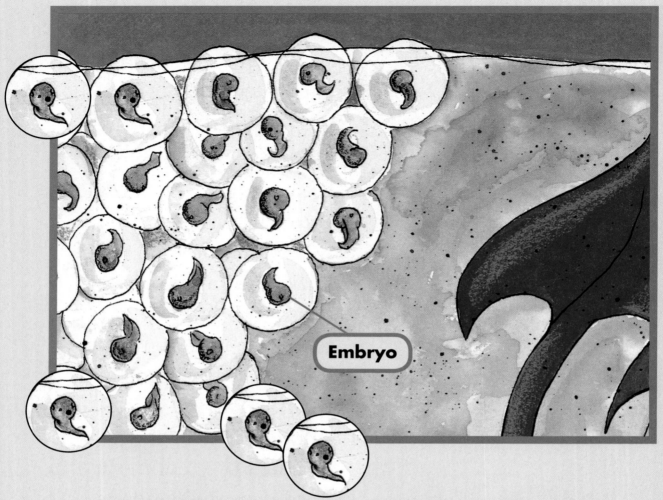

Embryo

The dark centers of the eggs slowly grow into frog embryos. The embryos grow until they look like small tadpoles. Tadpoles are frog babies. As they grow, they feed off their own egg yolks.

The tadpoles grow until they are big enough to break free into the water. It can take from three days to three weeks for this to happen, depending on what kind of frogs they will become.

One by one the tadpoles hatch from their eggs. They each have a head, tail, and body. The tadpoles wiggle their tails to swim.

The tadpoles breathe by getting air from the water through feathery outside gills. As they swim, they eat very small plants that stick to larger water plants. These tiny plants are called algae.

Tadpole

Head   Body   Tail

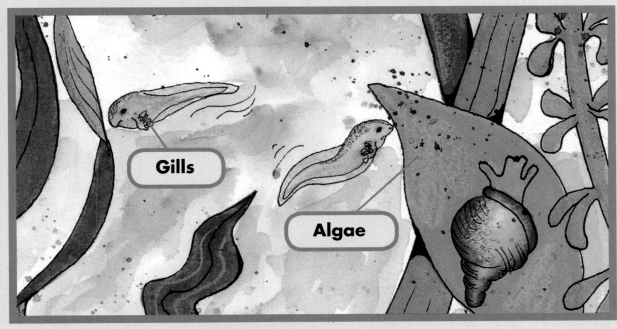

Gills

Algae

One week later the tadpoles look different. They are bigger. Their gills begin to shrink. A flap of skin slowly grows over them. The tadpoles' mouths become hard with tiny teeth in their upper jaws.

Now the tadpoles are one month old. Their outside gills have disappeared. New gills inside the tadpoles take oxygen from the water. Their tails are wider for stronger swimming. Something wonderful begins to happen. At the base of their tails, bulges appear. This is where their hind frog legs are growing.

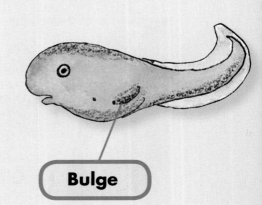

Bulge

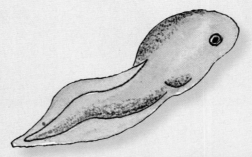

At two months old the tadpoles dart about the pond as they eat. They are still vegetarians. Vegetarians only eat plant life. The tadpoles get bigger. Now they have hind legs. Behind their heads bulges appear where their front legs are growing.

Their tails become smaller. The tadpoles' gills inside their bodies are gone. They have grown lungs to use for breathing. Now and then, they wiggle to the surface to breathe in air.

Bulge

Hind Legs

The tadpoles are about three months old. Again, they look different. They have front legs. Their tails are even smaller. They have shed their tadpole skin and lips. At last, they have the wide mouths of frogs.

The tadpoles have become tiny frogs. They climb out of the pond and onto the land. Their tails will become smaller and smaller until they finally disappear. The tiny frogs begin to eat insects and worms. They aren't vegetarians anymore.

Front Legs

Frog

Frogs are amphibians. The word *amphibian* comes from a Greek word that means "two lives." An amphibian can live on land or in the water.

Frogs are cold-blooded. That means their inside body temperatures are about the same as the outside temperature. During the next few years, the tiny frogs will grow to be mature frogs. Then they will be able to make their own frog spawn, and there will be new baby frogs.

Frogs have many body parts.

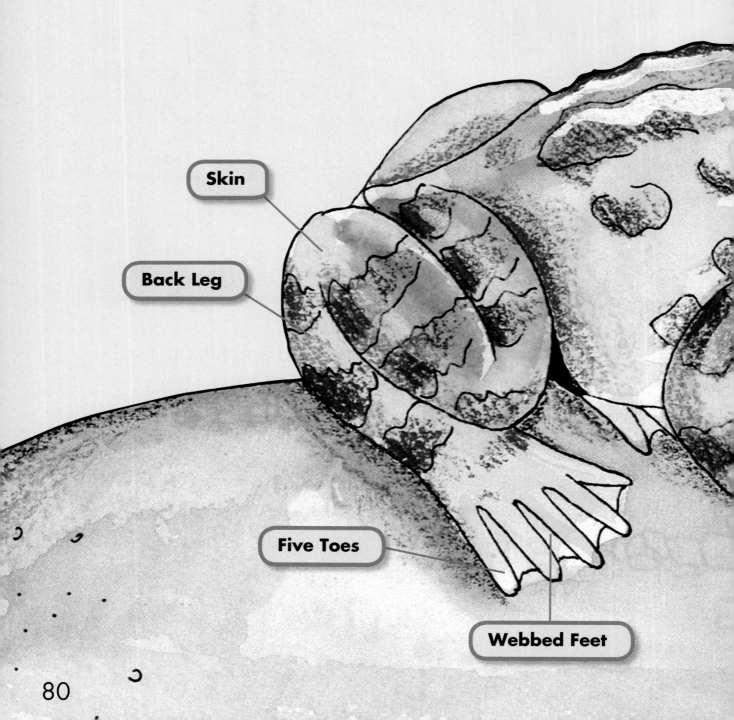

Skin

Back Leg

Five Toes

Webbed Feet

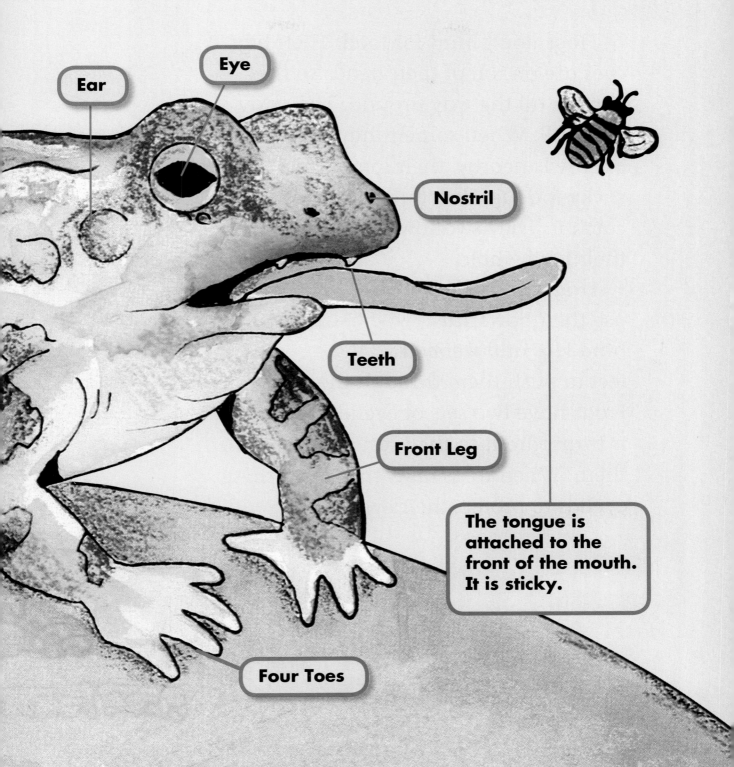

Ear

Eye

Nostril

Teeth

Front Leg

The tongue is attached to the front of the mouth. It is sticky.

Four Toes

Frogs don't hunt for food. Their big eyes are on top of their heads so they can see all the way around. They stay very still. When something flies or crawls nearby, their long, sticky tongues dart out to catch it. They swallow their food whole.

Frogs that swim use their powerful hind legs and webbed feet to push them through the water. Frogs have two sets of eyelids. One set is transparent so they can see through them. When frogs dive, they close these eyelids to protect their eyes.

On land, the frogs hop about. They use their very strong hind legs to leap. Most frogs can jump ten times their body length. They are wonderful jumpers!

The Difference Between a Frog and a Toad

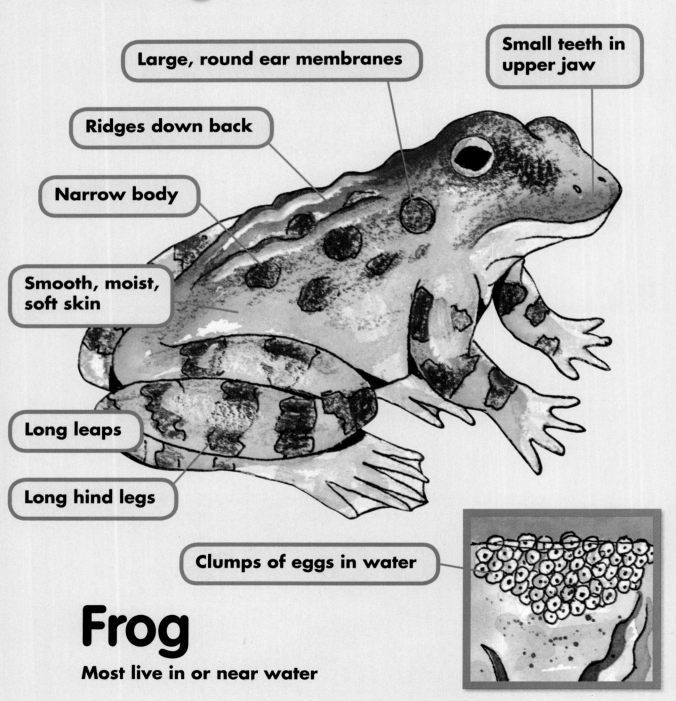

Large, round ear membranes

Small teeth in upper jaw

Ridges down back

Narrow body

Smooth, moist, soft skin

Long leaps

Long hind legs

Clumps of eggs in water

Frog
Most live in or near water

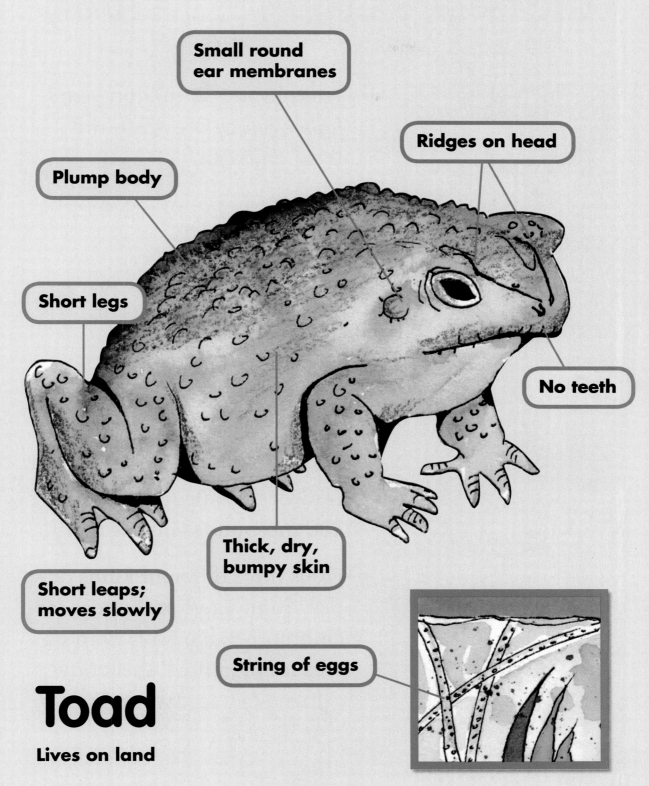

Small round
ear membranes

Ridges on head

Plump body

Short legs

No teeth

Thick, dry,
bumpy skin

Short leaps;
moves slowly

String of eggs

Toad

Lives on land

Croak . . . Croak . . . Croak

- Frogs lived 230 million years ago, even before dinosaurs lived on Earth.

- An African bullfrog can be as big as a football.

- Frogs protect gardens by eating huge amounts of insects.

- Some people eat frog legs, which they consider a delicacy.

- A dwarf puddle frog can eat 100 mosquitoes in one night.

- Frogs have different kinds of feet. Some have sticky toes for climbing. Some have pointed toes for digging. Others have webbed feet for swimming.

- Some tree frogs spend their entire lives in tree tops and never come down to the ground.

- The glass frog has strange skin. You can see through the skin to its insides.

- Some very big frogs can eat mice and rats.

- Some species of frogs are becoming extinct. Herpetologists are trying to find out what is causing this. We must learn to take better care of life on our planet.

Reader Response

Open for Discussion Be a teacher. Tell and draw how frog eggs become tadpoles, how tadpoles become tiny frogs, and how tiny frogs become mature frogs.

1. Gail Gibbons draws and tells at the same time. See how carefully her pictures go along with her words. Explain some examples.

2. Compare and contrast the way a frog looks after it comes out of the egg with when it hops on land.

3. Make a Venn diagram or some other graphic organizer to show the differences between a frog and a toad.

4. *Wiggles* and *shed* are action words that tell what a tadpole does. Find other action words in the story to add to the list.

Look Back and Write Look back at page 83. How far can a four-inch frog jump? How do you know? Use information from the selection to support your answer.

Gail Gibbons

Read two other books by Gail Gibbons.

Gail Gibbons likes to ask questions. She says, "The type of books I write are nonfiction books. This is because I love researching so much. I get to ask lots of questions, just like when I was a kid." Ms. Gibbons also loves traveling and meeting interesting people as she researches her books.

Ms. Gibbons and her husband live in Vermont. Their home is deep in the woods, surrounded by a lot of wild animals!

Puff . . . Flash . . . Bang!

Deadline! From News to Newspaper

89

Narrative Nonfiction

Genre

- Narrative nonfiction gives facts about real things.

- Narrative nonfiction is written more like a story than a list of facts.

Text Features

- The information in this selection is in short, descriptive paragraphs.

- The pictures provide more information.

Link to Science

Use the library or the Internet to find out more information about grasshoppers. Make a poster showing interesting facts you find.

From Egg to Egg

from *Life Cycles*

by Michael Elsohn Ross
illustrated by Gustav Moore

One warm May afternoon, a little head pokes out from a tiny egg hidden in the ground.

It's a baby grasshopper beginning its life cycle. Though she is smaller than a sunflower seed, she is as hungry as a lion. With her sharp jaws she munches leaves and grows.

She grows so much that soon she must crawl out of her old skin and then wait for her new, bigger skin to harden. Each day she munches more and more leaves. Each day she grows.

 Compare and Contrast What interesting comparisons does the writer make?

As summer passes she sheds her skin two more times. Now she has little wing pads on her back and large hind legs that help her jump far away from hungry predators.

By the end of July, she sheds her skin once more. Now she has wings and a long egg-laying tube.

Later she lays her eggs and leaves them behind in the soft soil. In October the cold comes, and many plants lose their leaves. The grasshopper has no food and soon dies, but her eggs are protected in the ground. All winter they lie hidden under leaves and snow.

One May day a little head pokes out from a tiny egg. It's a baby grasshopper and the beginning of another grasshopper life cycle.

Reading Across Texts

From what you've read about the life cycles of frogs and grasshoppers, which do you find more interesting?

Writing Across Texts Write a paragraph telling why you think as you do.

Graphic Organizers A time line might help you remember the facts.

Adjectives That Compare

Add **-er** to an adjective to compare two persons, places, or things. Add **-est** to an adjective to compare three or more persons, places, or things.

small   small**er** small**est**

A tadpole is **smaller** than a frog.

Smaller compares only two things—a tadpole and a frog.

The African bullfrog is the **biggest** frog of all.

Biggest compares many frogs.

Write   Using Adjectives That Compare

1. Look on page 76. Find two adjectives that compare. Write them.

2. Look at the frog and the toad on pages 84 and 85. Write some sentences that compare them. Use adjectives that compare.

3. Look back at the selection. Write a few sentences to describe how the tadpole changed into a frog. Use adjectives that compare.

Theme and Plot

- Every story has one "big idea."

- You can use something from your own life to understand the big idea, or theme, of a story.

- A plot is what happens at the beginning, middle, and end of a story.

- A character's actions help make up the plot of a story.

Plot Story Map

| Beginning | → | Middle | → | End |

Strategy: Summarize

Active readers sum up to check their understanding. To sum up, tell what happened. Tell only the most important events.

Write

1. Read "The Best Summer." Make a story map like the one above. Use it to tell the plot.

2. Use your story map to write a summary of the story. Read your summary. Then write the big idea you get from the story.

The Best Summer

Tara and Crystal were drawing chalk pictures on the front sidewalk.

"Let's draw all the fun things we will do this summer!" Tara said. The girls made pictures of day camp, swimming, picnics, roller-skating, jumping rope, and ice cream. "This will be a great summer!" Crystal said. •

Skill This is the beginning of the story. What happens here?

The next week, something changed. Crystal fell down and broke her arm. Her arm was in a cast, and it hurt. Tara made her friend a get-well card.

"No picnics, no swimming," said Crystal. • "No day camp, no roller-skating, and no jumping rope. This will be a bad summer!"

Strategy Here is the middle of the story. Summing up here will help you keep track of what's happening.

Tara went to see Crystal every day. The two girls played games. They made a tent out of a blanket. They had a picnic on the floor. They talked and laughed.

The girls sat on the steps and ate ice cream cones. Crystal said, "You are my best friend, Tara. This is a good summer after all!"

trouble

block

strong

giant

fair

tears

chuckle

Remember

Try the strategy. Then, if you need more help, use your glossary or a dictionary.

Vocabulary Strategy
for Multiple-Meaning Words

Context Clues Suppose when you are reading, you see a word you know, but the meaning doesn't fit in the sentence. The word may have more than one meaning. For example, *tip* means "the end part," as in the tip of a finger. *Tip* also means "a useful hint."

1. Try the meaning you know. Does it make sense in the sentence?

2. If not, the word may have another meaning. Read on and look at nearby words. Can you figure out another meaning?

3. Try the new meaning in the sentence. Does it make sense?

Read "Moving Tips." Look for words that can have more than one meaning. Remember to use nearby words to figure out a new meaning.

Moving Tips

Most people don't like to move. They don't like the work and the mess. They don't like the changes they have to make. But here are some tips that can make moving less trouble.

1. Find out about the area you are moving to. Drive around the block. Look for a grocery store, the library, and other places that are important to you.

2. Give your new address and telephone number to your family and friends.

3. Hire strong movers. Don't try to pack and move everything yourself.

4. Put a giant label on every box that tells in which room the box belongs. Put a label on each room too.

5. Know that some things will go wrong. Maybe it's not fair, but it's true.

6. If you feel like bursting into tears, take a break. Remember, someday you will look back and chuckle about this.

Write

What would you tell a new friend who just moved to your neighborhood? Write at least three tips. Use words from the Words to Know list.

I Like Where I Am

by Jessica Harper

illustrated by G. Brian Karas

Genre A **narrative poem** tells a story with rhyme and rhythm.

What would make the boy say, "I like where I am"?

I've got Trouble. . . . . .
    I've got
        BIG TROUBLE . . . . . .

'Cause I'm sittin' in my house
    on Willow Street
And I love this house.
    I love this street.
A prettier house
    you'll never meet
And I like where I am.
Yes, I like where I am.

That's why I've got Trouble.

'Cause I'm just kinda, you know, sittin',
Just messin' around with Mimi's kitten.
That's Mimi over there,
    in the little red chair.
She's usually got food in her hair.
She's not even two,
    so it's really not fair
That she's got a kitten
    and I don't.

And I'm six.

104

Well, anyway . . .
I'm sittin' with a kitten
        and a piece of string,
Just listening to my mama sing:

"La la, la la, la la!"

And I like where I am.

pots

La la, la la, la la!

I'm sittin' around and a truck shows up
And it's all bright red, this giant truck,
With two big men,
    they're REALLY big men!
Eight feet tall, or nine or ten!
They say,

"Hi, son, can we come in, please?"

Two men, as big and strong as trees. . . .
They make me feel all wobbly-knees!
They say,
    "HI, SON!"
       and that means me,
And that means I've got Trouble. . . .

107

They say, **"Hey, son, it's moving day!"**
That's right, it's moving day.
They're gonna pick us up and take us away.
And I think (but I'm too scared to say),
Oh, why don't you just go away!
Take your truck and take your Trouble and
Move somebody else!

Move
somebody
else!

'Cause I like my room and I like my school,
And we live real close to a swimming pool,
And my best friend lives around the block.
Why move to a place called Little Rock
Anyway?

The two big men kinda chuckle at me,
With a **ho ho ho** and a **hee hee hee**.
My mama takes me on her knee
And sings a gentle song to me.
She rocks me back and forth.

"La la, la la, la la."

We watch the men walk back and forth
With a **ho ho ho** and a **hee hee hee**.
My tears drop down on Mama's knee.

111

They pack all our stuff in their truck—
There goes Mimi's rubber duck!
They take my bike and then my mama's.
Look! They've got my dad's pajamas!

"Everything goes!"
they say with glee,
With a **ho ho ho** and a **hee hee hee**,
And I know I've got Trouble!

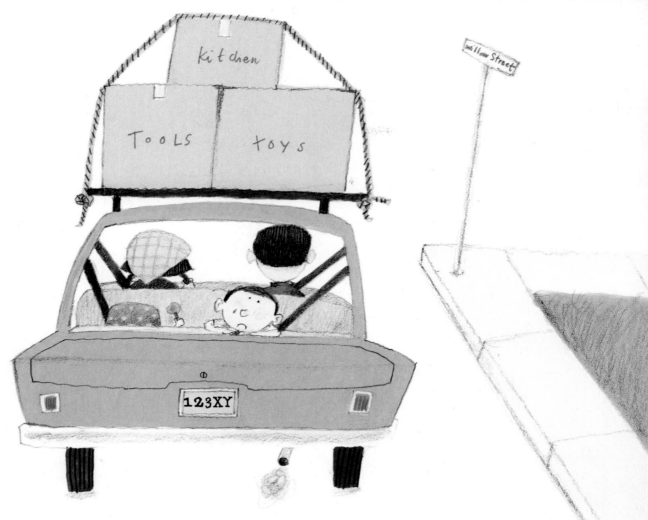

'Cause I like my room and I like my school.
We live real close to a swimming pool
And my best friend lives around the block.
Why move to a place called Little Rock
Anyway?

But we did . . . . . . just like that.

And guess what?

Do you know what?

We moved to a place called Little Rock
And my new friend lives
        just up the block!
He even has a swimming pool.
My room's okay and so's my school. . . .
And I've got my own kitten!

I still think of Willow Street.
The memory is very sweet.
I'll always love where I was born . . .
But when I wake up in the morning,
I like where I am!

With a **ho ho ho** and a **hee hee hee**.
I like where I am!

Reader Response

Open for Discussion Has anything like this happened to you or someone you know? What would you say to someone who is moving and does not want to move?

1. The author used words that bounce and rhyme. Which parts do you think show that bounce and rhyme? Read a part out loud.

2. What happened to the boy in the story? What do you think is the theme or big idea of the story?

3. Summarize how the boy reacted to the news about moving away.

4. Make a Venn diagram. Label the circles Old House and New House. Label the middle Both. Find words from the Words to Know list and the story to add to each circle.

Test Practice

Look Back and Write Look back at page 109. What did the boy pack in his boxes? How do you know?

Read other books written and illustrated by Jessica Harper and G. Brian Karas.

Jessica Harper moved twice as a child. "When I wrote this book about moving day, I recalled how it felt as a child to have my world taken apart and put back together again." Ms. Harper enjoys writing in rhyme. She says, "It's like solving a puzzle. What's the best way to say what I have to say *and* make it rhyme?"

I'm Not Going to Chase the Cat Today! by Jessica Harper

G. Brian Karas has illustrated many children's books. In elementary school, he was known as the "class artist."

Home on the Bayou: A Cowboy's Story by G. Brian Karas

E-Mail

Genre

- E-mail is short for "electronic mail." E-mail can be sent over the Internet from one computer to another.

- E-mail can be used to keep in touch with family and friends.

Text Features

- An e-mail message is like a friendly letter.

- It should have a greeting, a body, and a signature.

Link to Writing

Write a pretend e-mail message to a friend or relative. Tell about something that has changed for you.

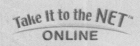

Take It to the NET™
ONLINE

more activities sfsuccessnet.com

A New House

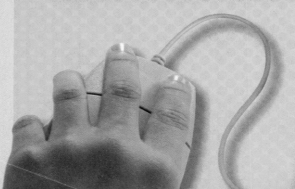

The boy in *I Like Where I Am* moved to a new home. Changes like this can be difficult but exciting.

Writing an e-mail message can help you keep in touch with family and friends far away. Here is how e-mail works.

When you turn on your computer and go into your e-mail, you can do these things.

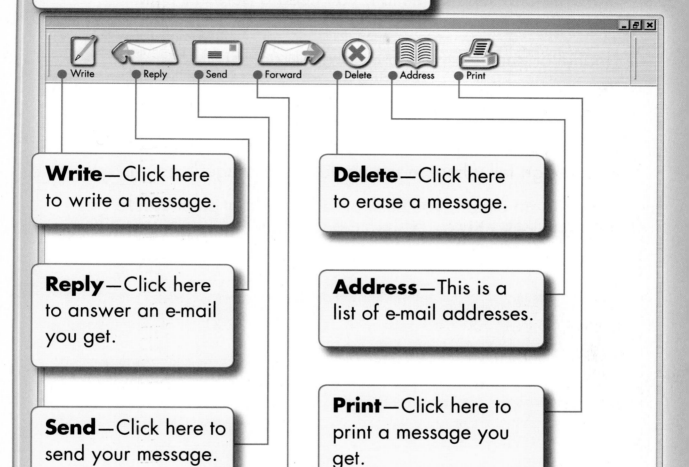

Write—Click here to write a message.

Reply—Click here to answer an e-mail you get.

Send—Click here to send your message.

Forward—Click here to send a message you get to someone else.

Delete—Click here to erase a message.

Address—This is a list of e-mail addresses.

Print—Click here to print a message you get.

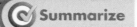 **Summarize** Summarize what you have read about e-mails.

119

How to Send E-mail

To write and send an e-mail, you need a person's e-mail address. E-mail addresses look like this:

(name of person)@(where message is going)

The letters on the left name the person or place you are writing to. People often use nicknames or abbreviations. The symbol @ stands for the word *at*. The letters to the right of the @ sign tell where in the world the message is going.

To write an e-mail, you click on a button that says **Write** or **Compose** or **New**. A new window will open that looks something like this:

To: You type the receiver's name here.

Subject: You type the subject of your message here. It is always best to fill this in.

Now you are ready to type your message, like the one on the next page.

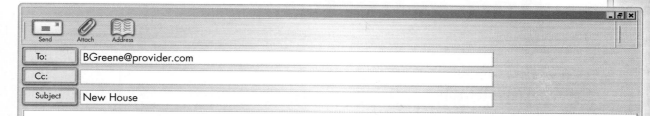

To: BGreene@provider.com

Cc:

Subject: New House

Hi, Beth!

What's new? If you asked me that, I'd have lots to tell you. Our new house is great. I didn't think I'd like it, but I do. I finally have my own room.

My new school is good too. I can walk and don't have to wait for a bus.

I miss you. Do you think you can come for a visit? Too bad you can't just run down the block anymore.

Your friend,

Colleen

Reading Across Texts

The boy in *I Like Where I Am* and Colleen both go through changes. Compare the changes of each.

Writing Across Texts Write an e-mail to one of them with advice about their changes.

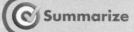 **Summarize** What have you learned about reading and writing e-mails?

Adverbs That Tell When and Where

Adverbs tell more about a verb. Some adverbs tell **when** or **where.**

Now two movers are at my house.

Now tells when.

The big men went **upstairs.**

Upstairs tells where.

Write Using Adverbs That Tell When and Where

1. Find a sentence in *I Like Where I Am* that uses an adverb to tell when or where. Write the sentence and underline the adverb.

2. The boy and his family are moving to Little Rock. What does he find there? Write two sentences. Use adverbs that tell when or where.

3. A postcard message is like a short letter. Your friend has moved away. Write a postcard message to your friend. Describe the things you miss doing together. Use adverbs that tell when or where.

Skill

Fact and Opinion

- A statement of fact can be proved true or false.

- A statement of opinion tells what someone thinks or feels.

Fact	Opinion

Strategy

Strategy: Ask Questions

Active readers ask themselves questions as they read. This gives you a purpose for reading and helps you identify facts and opinion.

1. Read "A Dog Named Ginger." Make a chart like the one above. Write two facts you read. Write two opinions.

2. Write a question you have about Ginger. Will the answer to your question be a fact or an opinion?

A Dog Named Ginger

Ginger is a very special dog. She is a guide dog. She helps people who cannot see. A mark in her ear and a tag on her collar show that she is a special working dog.

Ginger went to a training school. She learned how to walk on a lead, or stiff handle. She learned to listen. When Ginger walked with her teacher, no one could pet her, feed her, or play with her. She learned how to cross the street safely. She learned how to go around people. She learned to lead through doors and up and down steps. Ginger was the best dog in her school.

Now Ginger is never afraid. She can go where her owner goes. She can ride on a bus or on a train. She can go to work and to school. She helps her owner go all around. Ginger is the best dog in the world!

Skill Here is one fact and one opinion. *Ginger is a guide dog.* That can be proved. But whether she is special is only what one person thinks.

Strategy Here is a good place to ask a question: How do I know Ginger was the best dog in her school? Is this a fact or an opinion?

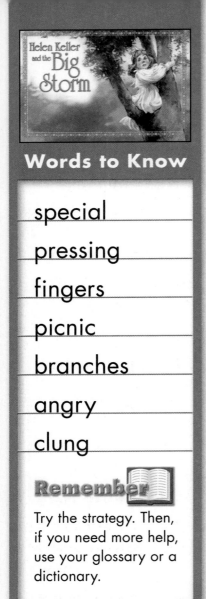

Words to Know

special
pressing
fingers
picnic
branches
angry
clung

Remember

Try the strategy. Then, if you need more help, use your glossary or a dictionary.

Vocabulary Strategy
for Multiple-Meaning Words

Context Clues During reading, you might come across a word you know, but the meaning doesn't fit in the sentence. The word may have more than one meaning. For example, *bank* means "a place to keep money." *Bank* also means "the ground along a river." You can use the other words around the word to figure out its meaning.

1. If the meaning you know doesn't make sense in the sentence, the word may have another meaning.

2. Read on and look at the words around this word. Can you figure out another meaning?

3. Try the new meaning in the sentence. Does it make sense?

As you read "Amy and Jake," look for words that can have more than one meaning. Remember to use nearby words to figure out a new meaning.

Amy and Jake

Amy and Jake are special friends. Each can do things that the other cannot. Amy can play the flute. She shows Jake how she does it—by pressing her fingers over the holes and blowing across the mouthpiece. Jake can read braille. He shows Amy how he does it—by sliding his fingers over the raised dots.

Last summer Amy and Jake went on a picnic in the woods. Amy helped Jake climb a tree. She gave him a boost and told him where to grab the branches. As they sat in the tree together, Amy described what she saw. Jake described what he felt and heard. So it was Jake who warned Amy about the angry bees. He heard them coming long before Amy did. Amy jumped down out of the tree and helped Jake down. Jake clung to Amy's hand as the two of them ran out of the woods. They had to jump into the pond to get away from the bees. They laugh about it now, but it was not so funny at the time.

Write

Write about something you and a friend do together. How do you help each other? Use words from the Words to Know list.

My friend Luis and I like to do special things. We like to have a picnic in the park.

Helen Keller and the Big Storm

by Patricia Lakin
illustrated by Troy Howell

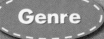 **Genre**   **Narrative nonfiction** tells the story of true events. Read about a true event from the life of Helen Keller.

What lesson does
Helen learn?

Little Helen Keller loved smelling roses and honeysuckle. They grew all around her Alabama home. But most of all, Helen loved playing pranks. When she was six, she had done her best prank yet! Mamma had walked into the kitchen pantry. Quickly, Helen felt for the key. *Click!*

Helen locked Mamma inside. Helen didn't always have the chance to take charge like that. Mamma and Papa tried hard to understand her. But many times no one knew what she wanted.

Helen could get so angry, she would kick and hit and fall into a heap. Afterward, she ran outside. She threw herself onto the cool, comforting grass. The flowers, trees, grass, warm sun, and gentle wind always made Helen feel better.

Helen was never punished for her pranks and tantrums. Mr. and Mrs. Keller thought Helen had been punished enough. Their daughter could not hear, or see, or talk. But that pantry prank forever changed Helen's life. The Kellers now knew that Helen needed more than they could give her. She needed special lessons from a special teacher.

Helen's teacher was Annie Sullivan. She came to live with the Kellers. Helen was not ready to trust this stranger. And she was not ready to give up her pranks. She locked Annie inside her room. And this time Helen hid the key! That prank made Annie see just how clever Helen was. No matter what Helen did, Annie did not give up!

Slowly, day by day, she worked with Helen. Annie taught Helen by pressing her fingers into Helen's hand. Annie's fingers spelled out the names for the things Helen loved. Grass. Flowers. Leaves. Trees. Bugs. Butterflies. Sun. Wind. Rain. In a short time, Helen loved doing her lessons more than doing her pranks.

Soon, the out-of-doors became Helen's classroom. One summer day, Helen and Annie took a long walk. On their way home, the air grew hot and sticky. Helen and Annie stopped to rest under a wild cherry tree. The tree blocked them from the burning hot sun. Its leaves fanned them with a gentle, cooling breeze.

Helen felt its strong, low branches. They were just right for climbing. Annie and Helen decided to do just that! Sitting high in the tree, they had a resting place to stay cool. It was a perfect spot for a picnic!

Annie headed for the house to make the lunch. She made Helen promise not to move an inch. Helen wouldn't think of moving. She loved sitting high up in that tree! Helen breathed in the wonderful scent of the cherry tree. She stroked its rough bark and its smooth green leaves. She let the cooling breeze blanket her.

But in seconds, Helen's world turned upside down. The sun disappeared. Helen's face was slapped with a cold, sharp wind.

The scent of flowers was gone. Her nose was filled with another smell. This one was not sweet. It came up from the deep, dark earth. It told Helen that a storm was near. Helen began to feel the shaking of the leaves. Twigs rained down, scratching her face, arms, and legs.

Tree limbs swayed. The wind whipped through the branches. The wind whipped around Helen. The wind tried to rip Helen right out of that tree. Helen grabbed onto the shaking branch. She clung to it with all of her might. Helen sat frozen.

She was trapped. She could not see. She could not call for help. She could not hear if help was on the way. Helen had never felt so alone or so scared. She couldn't understand how the gentle things she loved could turn against her.

Suddenly, out of the cold, whipping wind, Helen felt a hand. It was a strong, warm hand. It belonged to Annie Sullivan. Annie grabbed hold of Helen. Helen let go of the branch. She clung to Annie. She let Annie guide her down and out of that tree.

Helen learned a great deal that day. She had felt the power of Nature. It could turn from gentle to fierce in seconds. Helen also learned about the power of friendship. Annie Sullivan would always be there for Helen Keller.

Helen Keller and Annie Sullivan were friends all of their lives. Helen went on to become a talented writer who always worked to help others.

Reader Response

Open for Discussion On page 137, the author says, "Helen's world turned upside down." What does that mean? Explain why you think the author said that.

1. Helen Keller really lived. The big storm really happened. How do you think the author found out about Helen Keller and the big storm?

2. Annie Sullivan was Helen's teacher. Is that a statement of fact or opinion? How do you know?

3. What questions did you ask yourself as you read? How did that help you?

4. The author often uses two words to describe something in nature. Work with a partner. Find the noun that each pair of words describes: *hot, sticky; burning, hot; gentle, cooling; strong, low; smooth, green; cold, sharp; deep, dark.*

Look Back and Write The author tells you what Helen learned that day. What two things did she learn? Look at page 140. Use details from the selection in your answer.

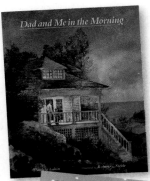

Read more books by Patricia Lakin.

Patricia Lakin never saw herself as a writer. "I never thought I could write." Then Ms. Lakin took a writing class. She was told to write about things she cared about. Writing was fun for the first time.

Ms. Lakin wrote *Helen Keller and the Big Storm* because Helen had so many things to overcome. "Nature was a source of comfort for her." After being caught in the storm, Helen was shocked "to learn that nature could also be so strong and dangerous."

Dad and Me in the Morning

Snow Day!

143

Expository Nonfiction

Genre

- **Expository nonfiction explains an idea about the real world.**
- **It gives facts about the topic.**

Text Features

- **Expository nonfiction often uses photos and diagrams to help the reader understand the topic.**

Link to Science

Use an encyclopedia or the Internet to find out more about hurricanes or tornadoes. Draw a diagram that shows how the storm forms. Label your diagram.

Wind

by Marion Dane Bauer

The Earth we live on is a spinning ball. When Earth spins, the air around it moves too.

144

When air moves, we call it "wind." As the sun heats the air, the air grows lighter. Light air rises.

Cool air is heavy. It falls. Cool air and warm air are always trading places. We call this movement "wind."

Birds use wind to help them fly. Plants use wind to carry their seeds.

Ask Questions If you don't understand, ask yourself a question.

We use wind to fly kites, to sail boats, and to turn windmills.

Wind moves clouds. Wind makes waves. It even makes trees bend. When the hot air is very light and the cold air is very heavy, wind can blow up a storm!

146

Sometimes wind spins like a puppy chasing its tail. A small spin makes a dust devil or a water spout. A strong spin makes a tornado or a hurricane.

dust devil

view of hurricane from space

tornado

Wind can be scary. Or it can sing a gentle song. Wind is all around us, but we cannot see it. We can only see what wind does.

Reading Across Texts
In "Wind," you read: "Wind can be scary. Or it can sing a gentle song." Was that true in *Helen Keller and the Big Storm*?

Writing Across Texts
Write a short paragraph explaining your answer.

Fact and Opinion Find a fact about wind. Find an opinion.

147

Adverbs That Tell How

An **adverb** can tell more about a verb by telling how an action is done. **Adverbs** that tell how usually end in **-ly**.

Quickly, Helen felt for the key.

The word **quickly** tells how Helen felt for the key.

When she was angry, Helen would kick **wildly**.

The word **wildly** tells how Helen kicked.

Write Using Adverbs That Tell How

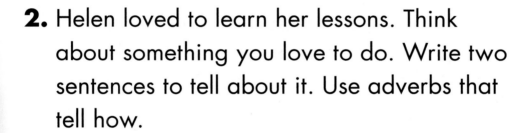

1. Find a sentence in the story that uses an adverb to tell how. Write the sentence. Underline the adverb.

• •

2. Helen loved to learn her lessons. Think about something you love to do. Write two sentences to tell about it. Use adverbs that tell how.

• •

3. Think of something you have done that was fun or made you happy. Write some sentences about it. Use adverbs that tell how.

Time Line of My Life

connect to
WRITING

Think about some of the most important events in your life. Write a sentence about each one on an index card. Draw a picture to go with your sentence. Then attach the cards in order to a piece of yarn. Use clothespins or paper clips.

I was born on September 23.

We got Sparky our dog in December.

My brother Timmy was born on April 9, 2003.

Life Cycles

connect to
SCIENCE

You learned about the life cycles of frogs, grasshoppers, and pumpkins in Unit 4. Choose one of these or another plant or animal. Make a circle diagram. Show the different stages of the life of this plant or animal. Write a label for each stage.

Memory Quilt

connect to
ART

With a group, list some special events that have happened in school so far this year. Each person can choose one event. Use cut paper and paste to make a quilt square to remember the event. Combine your quilt square with ones made by others in the class.

151

Responsibility

What does it mean to be responsible?

Read It
ONLINE
sfsuccessnet.com

 connect to **SOCIAL STUDIES**

Firefighter!
Firefighters have an important job in the community.

Narrative Nonfiction

 connect to **SCIENCE**

One Dark Night
A boy takes care of a stray cat and her kittens.

Realistic Fiction

 connect to **SOCIAL STUDIES**

Bad Dog, Dodger!
Sam is responsible for his pet's behavior.

Realistic Fiction

 connect to **SOCIAL STUDIES**

Horace and Morris but mostly Dolores
Good friends take care of their friendship.

Fantasy

 connect to **SOCIAL STUDIES**

The Signmaker's Assistant
A young signmaker takes responsibility for his actions.

Humorous Fiction

Main Idea

- The main idea is the most important idea in a selection.

- The main idea is often stated near the beginning of a selection.

- Details tell more about the main idea.

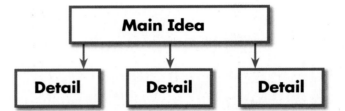

 Strategy: Text Structure

Text structure is the way a selection is organized. A selection can be organized in the order in which things happen. Noticing the organization can help you find the main idea.

1. Read "My Uncle, the Firefighter." Find the main idea and at least three details.

2. Make a graphic organizer like the one above. Fill it in with the main idea and details you found.

My Uncle, the Firefighter

My Uncle Ernie works hard as a firefighter in our town. He puts out brush fires and house fires. He helps at car wrecks. He saves people.

One morning, Uncle Ernie took me to the fire station. I saw the hose truck and the ladder truck. Uncle Ernie and the other firefighters had a drill. They practiced with the hoses.

Next, Uncle Ernie let me try on his heavy coat, helmet, and boots. I got to stand on the back of the fire truck!

I had a great time. My Uncle Ernie is good at his job. He is a great firefighter.

Skill Here's the main idea of this paragraph. What is it? Read on to find some details.

Strategy How is this selection organized? In what order did things happen?

Vocabulary Strategy

for Suffixes

Word Structure Sometimes when you are reading, you may come across a word you don't know. Look closely at the word. Does it have *-ly* at the end? When the suffix *-ly* is added to a word, it usually makes the word mean "in a ___ way." For example, *kindly* means "in a kind way." Use the *-ly* suffix to help you figure out the meaning of the word.

1. Put your finger over the *-ly* suffix.

2. Look at the base word. Put the base word in the phrase "in a ___ way."

3. Try that meaning in the sentence. Does it make sense?

Read "A Trip to the Fire Station." Look for words that end with *-ly*. Use the suffix to help you figure out the meanings of the words.

A Trip to
the Fire Station

Carlos is a firefighter. Some children are at his fire station for a tour. He points out where the firefighters sleep and eat. Carlos slides down the fire pole. "That is how we quickly get from our beds to the trucks," he says.

"We use hoses to spray water on a fire," he says. "Fire hoses can be very heavy when they are filled with water. We have to grip the hoses tightly."

"Fires give off a lot of smoke," Carlos tells the children. "We must wear air tanks and masks if we go into a fire. We use masks to breathe clean air."

Carlos shows the children his thick clothes, heavy boots, and hard helmet. "These keep me safe from the things that can fall from or in a burning building."

Suddenly, the fire alarm goes off! Carlos tells the children good-by. He puts on his gear and climbs onto the fire truck. With a loud roar, the fire truck races off.

Write

What might happen to Carlos next? Write more of the story. Use words from the Words to Know list.

Narrative nonfiction tells about a true event or a series of events. Look for true events in the day of a firefighter.

Fire Fighter!

by Angela Royston

How hard is a firefighter's job?

It is busy at the fire station even when there is no fire. Liz is checking the hoses. She wants to make sure they screw tightly to the truck.

Dan is polishing the fire truck wheels. Anthony is upstairs in the kitchen, looking for a snack. He is always hungry! Suddenly a loud noise makes him jump.

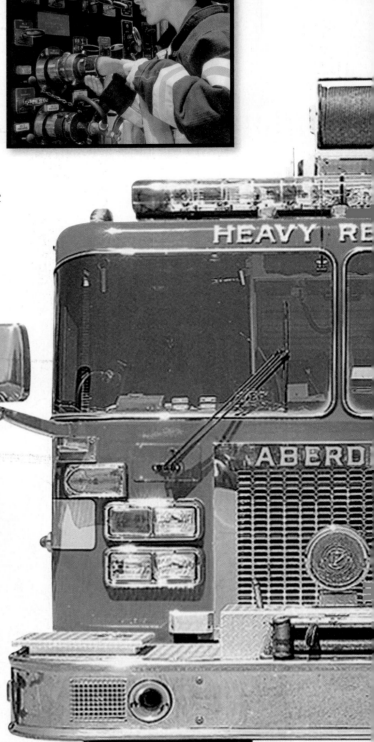

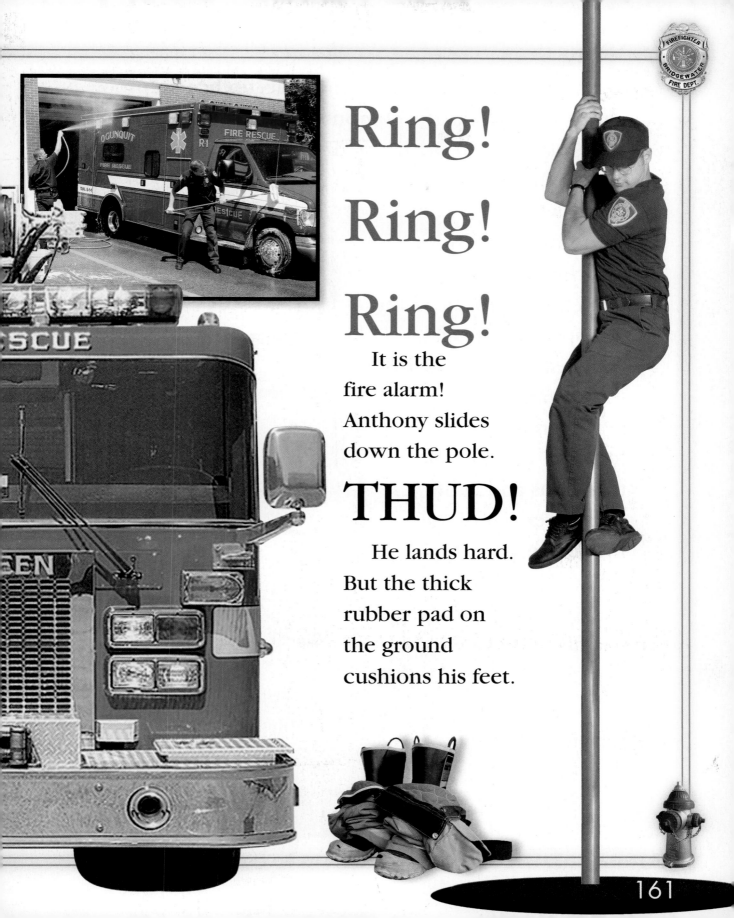

Ring!

Ring!

Ring!

It is the
fire alarm!
Anthony slides
down the pole.

THUD!

He lands hard.
But the thick
rubber pad on
the ground
cushions his feet.

Liz jumps into her boots and pulls up her fireproof pants. She checks the computer. It shows the fire is at 7 Oak Lane. In the truck Liz grabs the walkie-talkie. "Chief Miller! We're on our way!"

"Right!" says the fire chief.

He has gone ahead in a special fast car. "I'll meet you there."

Liz starts the engine as the firefighters jump in. She flips on the sirens and lights and drives out of the fire house. The truck speeds toward the fire.

Cars and buses stop and wait when they hear the siren coming.

The fire chief calls Liz. "I'm at the fire scene. It's an old house that's been empty for years. But someone saw a young boy playing on the porch this morning. He might be inside the house. Tell Dan and Anthony to get their air tanks ready."

"Okay, Chief," says Liz. "I can see the smoke from here. We'll be there in two minutes."

Liz turns the corner into Oak Lane. Flames cover the top of the house.

The fire is spreading quickly. There's no time to lose! Liz hooks a hose from the truck to the nearest fire hydrant. A pump on the truck pulls water from the hydrant to another hose. Liz and another firefighter point the hose at the flames. "Ready!" calls Liz.

WHOOSH!

They hold on tight as the water shoots out. It comes out of a fire hose hard enough to knock a person down.

Anthony and Dan are ready to search the burning building. They have put on their air tanks and face masks. Each tank holds 40 minutes of air. That's not much time!

"The boy's name is Luke," the chief tells them.

"Right," says Anthony. He grabs a hose.

"Let's put the wet stuff on the red stuff!" says Dan.

Dan and Anthony run to the back of the house. The fire is not as bad here. Dan feels the back door. If it is hot, flames could leap out. "It's cold," says Dan. They step inside.

Thick black smoke is everywhere. Anthony shines his flashlight around. "Luke! Luke!" he calls. No one answers.

"I can hear fire upstairs," says Dan.

The fire has damaged the staircase. It could fall down at any time. They climb up the steps very slowly.

167

Outside, the outriggers are set down on the ground. Outriggers are like legs. They keep the truck steady as the ladder is raised. The ladder goes up like a telescope to the top of the house. A hose runs up the side. The firefighter on the ladder shoots water down on the fire. The flames crackle and hiss. They get smaller, then suddenly jump even higher.

Inside the house, the fire rages. It is hot enough to melt glass. Anthony sprays water on the flames. Fire has made the house weak.

"It could come down any second," says Dan. "We must find Luke."

BOOM! A beam crashes down near them. But their helmets protect their heads. CRASH!

"Quick!" says Anthony. "We're running out of time."

They come to another door. But it will not open. Dan swings his ax at the door. Once. Twice. Three times. "It's jammed!" shouts Dan. The roar of the fire is so loud they can hardly hear. "We'll have to use the electric saw."

Anthony switches on the saw. WHRRR! He cuts a hole in the door big enough to climb through.

"Luke!" calls Dan. "Luke?" But the room is empty.

Suddenly the chief calls. "Get out now! The roof is coming down!"

Dan and Anthony race downstairs. They get out just as the roof falls in. "We didn't find Luke!" yells Dan.

"He's okay," says the chief. "We just found him up the block."

"Whew!" says Dan. "Good news!"

Hours later the flames are out. Anthony sprays water on the parts still glowing red. He is tired and dirty—and very hungry!

Liz winds the hoses back on to the truck. Finally she rests. She is tired too. Back at the station Anthony sits down to eat. "At last!" he says.

Suddenly a loud noise makes him jump.

"Dinner will have to wait!" laughs Dan.

Ring! Ring! Ring!

Practice E.D.I.T.H.—Exit Drills in the Home

Do you know what to do if a fire starts in your home? Don't wait until it happens:

- Sit down with your family now.

- Talk about how you would get out of the house.

- Plan at least two ways out of every room.

- Decide where you will all meet once you get outside.

A fire drill now could save lives later!

Reader Response

Open for Discussion Firefighter Dan says, "Let's put the wet stuff on the red stuff!" Pretend you are there. Tell everything you hear, smell, and see.

1. The author has reasons for writing *Firefighter!* for you to read. What do you think those reasons are?

2. On pages 162–163 of *Firefighter!*, what important idea is the author trying to tell you?

3. The author wrote about an actual fire. How did the order of events the author told about help you understand the information?

4. Write a letter to your local newspaper telling them why your neighborhood fire station should win an award. Use some of the words from the Words to Know list.

Look Back and Write Firefighters need equipment—things to help them fight fires. Look through the story. Find at least ten pieces of equipment used by firefighters. Write them in a list.

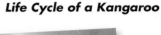

Angela Royston

Read two more books by Angela Royston.

Angela Royston writes books about all sorts of things. She has written about animals, plants, ships, trains, trucks, cars, and science. Royston was born in England and studied many different things at school. "I feel able to tackle almost any subject," she says. "I most like to work on books that are fun." She likes to read all she can about something before she writes about it.

Life Cycle of a Kangaroo

Strange Plants

173

Drama
in Reading

Play

Genre
- A play is a story that is acted out.
- A play has characters who each have their own speaking parts.

Text Features
- A character's name appears before each speaking part.
- Directions to the actors sometimes appear in parentheses. These tell the actors how to move, where to go, or what to do.

Link to Reading
Use the library to find other plays to read. Choose one or two to read together as a Readers' Theater.

FIRE FIGHTING

TEAMWORK

a play by Connie Carpenter

CHARACTERS:

Firefighter Kelly (FF KELLY)

Firefighter Sanchez (FF SANCHEZ)

Firefighter Johnson (FF JOHNSON)

Chief

Three or Four Council Members

Scene: A firehouse.
(One firefighter is sweeping. Another is washing dishes. Another is sleeping.)

FF KELLY: *(sweeping)* Boy, is this fire station dirty!

FF SANCHEZ: *(washing dishes)* Yeah, we all have to clean up the mud and dirt we tracked in. That last fire was a mess!

FF KELLY: I think Johnson worked really hard. He had to roll up that hose almost all by himself. That was hard work! He's probably upstairs taking a nap.
(Telephone rings.)

FF KELLY: *(stops sweeping)* I'll get that. *(picks up phone)* Firefighter Kelly here.

CHIEF: *(voice from off stage)* Firefighter Kelly, this is the Chief.

FF KELLY: Yes, Chief. What is it?

CHIEF: We're having an inspection by the city council today. Is everything in shape?

FF KELLY: It will be, Chief. With teamwork we should be able to get things in tip-top shape for the inspection.

CHIEF: Good! I'll bring the council right over.

FF KELLY: Right! Good-by, Chief! *(hangs up phone)* We've got big trouble!

Ⓒ Main Idea   Sum up the main idea so far.

FF SANCHEZ: What? Is it a fire? an accident?

FF KELLY: No! The Chief is bringing over the city council for an inspection.

FF SANCHEZ: Uh-oh! We'd better hurry!

FF KELLY: What about our beds?

FF SANCHEZ: Johnson is up there. Do you think he made them?

FF KELLY: We'd better get up there and check! *(Both firefighters run up the stairs. Firefighter Johnson is lying on bed, snoring.)*

FF KELLY: *(looks at beds)* Just as I thought! Unmade!

FF SANCHEZ: Johnson, wake up!

FF JOHNSON: What? What is it? *(wakes up and rises)* What's happening?

FF SANCHEZ: *(begins making bed)* We have to hurry. The Chief is bringing the city council over for an inspection.

FF JOHNSON: Inspection! Oh, no! Let's get this place cleaned up. *(begins making bed)*

FF KELLY: I'll get the broom. This place needs sweeping. I'll use the pole. It's faster. *(slides down pole)*

Main Idea   What main idea is the author trying to get across?

(Fire alarm rings.)

FF JOHNSON: The alarm!

FF SANCHEZ: This cleaning will have to wait. *(Firefighters slide down pole and put on their gear. Firefighter Sanchez checks fireboard for location of fire and turns off alarm.)*

FF SANCHEZ: There! I've turned off the alarm. The fire is at 422 East Jay Street. Let's go! *(Firefighters exit; fire truck siren slowly fades away.) (Chief and council members arrive.)*

CHIEF: *(looking around)* This place looks great! Kelly, Johnson, Sanchez? *(Chief looks at fireboard to find out where the firefighters have gone. He turns to council members.)* It looks like they've gone to another fire. Well, that's our fire department. They're hard workers, both in the fire station and in the community.

Reading Across Texts
Each selection told of certain jobs firefighters must do. What did you learn about the jobs? Which job do you think is most important?

Writing Across Texts Write a brief paragraph to explain your answer.

Pronouns

A **pronoun** is a word that takes the place of a noun or nouns. The words **he, she, it, we, you,** and **they** are pronouns.

Liz starts the engine. **She** flips on the sirens and lights.

She takes the place of the noun **Liz**.

Anthony and **Dan** are ready to search the house. **They** have put on air tanks and face masks.

They takes the place of the nouns **Anthony** and **Dan**.

Write Using Pronouns

1. Find a sentence in the story that uses a noun. Write that sentence using a pronoun in place of the noun.

• •

2. What have you learned about firefighters? Write two sentences about them. Use two or three pronouns in your sentences.

• •

3. Reread page 171. Plan a poster to persuade your classmates to use E.D.I.T.H.—**E**xit **D**rills **i**n **t**he **H**ome. Use pronouns in place of some nouns.

Comprehension

Skill
Sequence

Strategy
Graphic
Organizers

 Skill

Sequence

- Sequence is the order of events in a story.

- Clue words such as *first, next, then, now,* and *finally* will help you figure out and remember the order of events.

 Strategy

Strategy: Graphic Organizers

A graphic organizer is a picture that can help you organize information as you read. You can make a graphic organizer like this one to show the order of events in a story.

First:
Next:
Then:
Now:
Finally:

 **Write**

1. Read "When a Thunderstorm Strikes." Write down some clue words that tell the order of events.

2. Make a graphic organizer like the one above. Fill in your chart to show the order of events as you read.

When a Thunderstorm Strikes

A thunderstorm can happen even on a nice day. First, you may see big dark clouds in the distance. They were not there an hour ago. You also see that the clouds are moving toward you.

Skill Here's a clue word. *First* tells you that events are beginning to happen.

The next thing you know—flash! Lightning streaks from the clouds to the ground. Then—boom! Thunder rumbles. You can tell how far away the storm is. Just count the seconds between the flash and the boom. Every five seconds is one mile. So, if you count five seconds, the storm is one mile away.

Strategy If you made a graphic organizer, use the clue word in this sentence to add more information to it.

Now the storm is moving closer. When you count fewer than five seconds between lightning and thunder, the storm is less than a mile away.

Finally, you can't count even one full second. The storm is here!

Words to Know

lightning

thunder

storm

flashes

rolling

pounds

pours

Remember

Try the strategy. Then, if you need more help, use your glossary or a dictionary.

Vocabulary Strategy

For Unfamiliar Words

Context Clues Sometimes as you read, you may not know the meaning of a word. What can you do? You can look at the words and sentences around the word. These are called **context clues**. They can help you figure out the meaning of the word you don't know.

1. Read the words and sentences around the word you don't know. Sometimes the author tells you what the word means.

2. Use the words and sentences to predict a meaning for the word.

3. Try that meaning in the sentence. Does it make sense?

Read "Some Like It Stormy." Use context clues to help you understand the meanings of the vocabulary words.

182

Some Like It Stormy

My cat Trevor is afraid of noises. He hates lightning and thunder. Whenever there is a storm, he hides in my bedroom closet. I usually go into the closet with him. I do that to keep him company, not because I am afraid. Only babies—and Trevor—are afraid of storms.

In fact, I like a good storm. I like the way lightning flashes and crackles like fireworks. It makes loud noises that boom in my ears. I like the way thunder crashes and rumbles. It sounds like rolling bowling balls. I like the way rain pounds on the ground and pours off the roofs of the houses. After the storm, the whole world smells fresh and new.

But try telling Trevor that. I have tried to explain storms to him. He always listens and seems to understand. But then the next time there is a storm, there he is, back in the closet again!

Write

Do you like storms? Write about how you feel about storms. Use words from the Words to Know list.

Genre **Realistic fiction** tells about events that could happen in real life. Could this story really happen?

184

One Dark Night

by Hazel Hutchins

illustrated by Susan Kathleen Hartung

What can happen on a rainy, dark night?

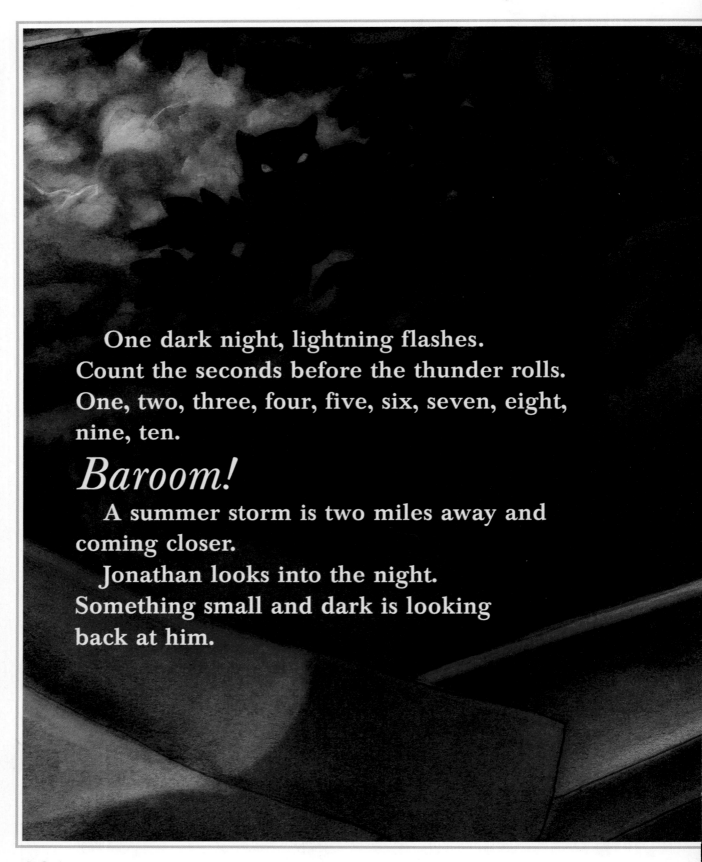

One dark night, lightning flashes.
Count the seconds before the thunder rolls.
One, two, three, four, five, six, seven, eight,
nine, ten.

Baroom!

A summer storm is two miles away and
coming closer.

Jonathan looks into the night.
Something small and dark is looking
back at him.

He races downstairs and
throws open the screen door.
"The stray cat's afraid of the
thunder!" he tells his grandparents.

"Stray cats aren't afraid of storms,"
says Grandfather.

"Look out! I think she's got a
mouse!" cries Grandmother.
But stray cat is already inside
and laying her prize on the rug.

"It's a kitten!" says Jonathan.
One small kitten—soft as whispers,
gray as dawn.

189

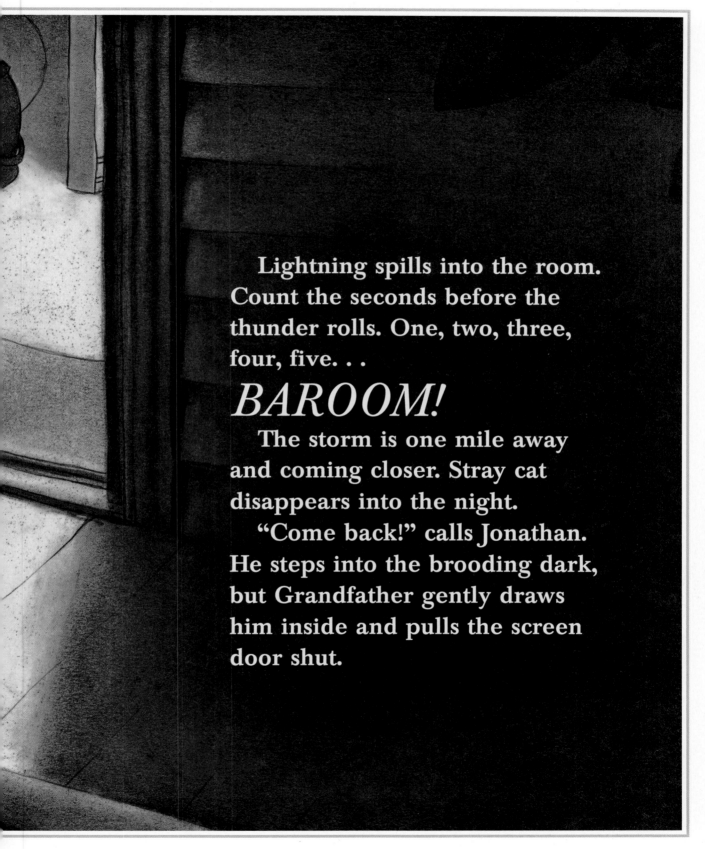

Lightning spills into the room. Count the seconds before the thunder rolls. One, two, three, four, five. . .

BAROOM!

The storm is one mile away and coming closer. Stray cat disappears into the night.

"Come back!" calls Jonathan. He steps into the brooding dark, but Grandfather gently draws him inside and pulls the screen door shut.

Jonathan lays his bathrobe on the rug.
He snuggles the kitten within its folds.
"We'll take care of it, won't we?" he asks.
   "As ever best we can," says Grandmother.
But how can they take care of anything so small?

A scratching at the door.
Two green eyes peer in at them.
   "She's back! She's back!"
cries Jonathan and races to the door.
   Stray cat enters, carrying a second
kitten–soft as stuffing, white as snow.
   Lightning flashes. Count the seconds
before the thunder rolls. One, two, thr–
BARRROOOMMM!
   The storm is half a mile away
and coming closer. Stray cat darts into
the night before the last echo fades.

Outside a great wind whips the trees
and hurtles single drops of rain.

Splat! Splat!

Jonathan warms the kittens in their bed
and looks into the night. Watching. Waiting.

This time when the lightning comes
it splits the sky with wild, white brightness.
There is no time to count before the
thunder cracks.

BAAAARRRROOOOM!

A hard rain drums the roof and pounds into
the grass like something angry.

"There she is!" cries Jonathan.

The next moment he is outside too,
to help them battle through the rain.
One boy, one cat, and a third small kitten—
wet as water, black as night. The rain pours.
Jonathan drips puddles on the floor.
"Are there any more?" he asks stray cat.
"Do we need another trip?"

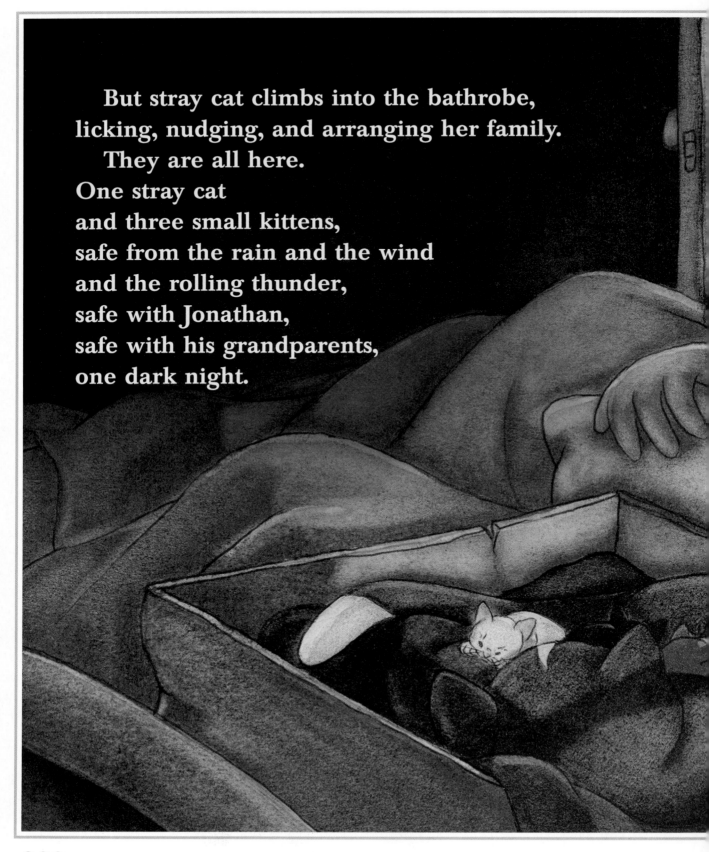

But stray cat climbs into the bathrobe,
licking, nudging, and arranging her family.
   They are all here.
One stray cat
and three small kittens,
safe from the rain and the wind
and the rolling thunder,
safe with Jonathan,
safe with his grandparents,
one dark night.

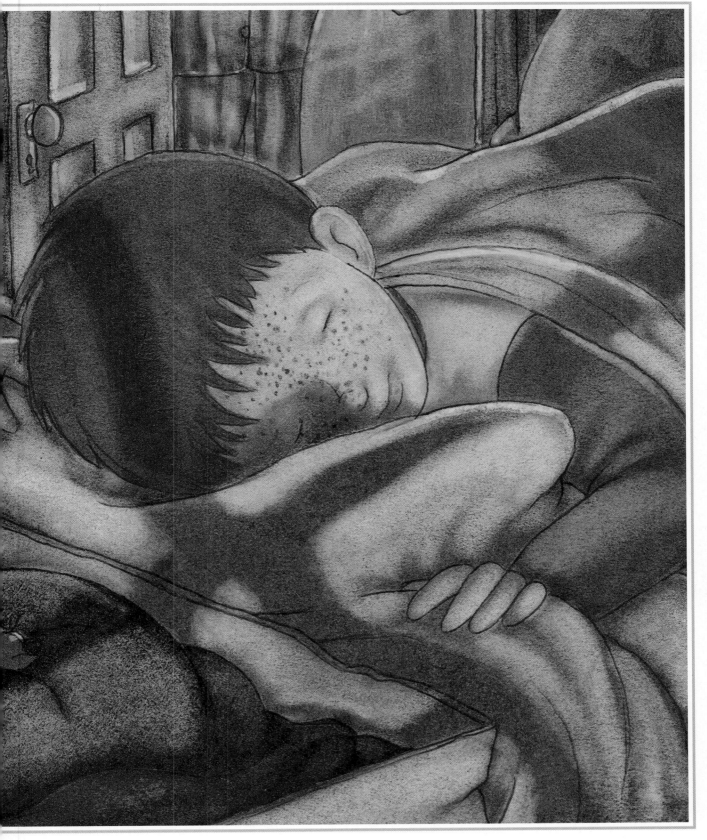

Reader Response

Open for Discussion A storm can be terrible or exciting! Read an exciting part aloud. Make your reading exciting! Tell why you picked that part.

1. How does the author use words to tell you how each kitten is different? Go back and find those words.

2. How did Jonathan know that the storm was getting closer? What was the first thing he noticed about the thunder and lightning? What did he notice next? after that?

3. Make a graphic organizer to tell what happened to the mother cat at the beginning, the middle, and the end of the story.

4. The storm in *One Dark Night* is loud and scary. Make a web with the word *storm* in the center. Add words from the Words to Know list and the story that describe the storm.

Look Back and Write On page 188, Jonathan, Grandfather, and Grandmother each say something about the stray cat. Are they right? Explain your answer.

One Duck

Two So Small

Hazel Hutchins lives in Canada. She wanted to be an author from the time she was ten years old. Now, she has written more than 25 books!

How did she get the idea for *One Dark Night*? Ms. Hutchins says, "People often tell me stories about their pets. Over the years, I have been told at least three stories about mother cats moving their kittens to a house or porch when threatened by a storm. I have always been touched by the stories as they express the safety we all seek for our loved ones at times of danger."

Ms. Hutchins loves to read books and write stories.

Genre

- **Poetry often has a rhythm or a beat. Listen for the beat as you read these poems.**

- **Sometimes poetry rhymes, but not always.**

- **Each stanza of "Adoption" has two rhyming lines. "The Stray Cat" uses rhyming words in different places throughout the poem.**

- **A poet often tries to create clear images with as few words as possible.**

Link to Writing

Write your own poem about a cat. Use rhyme and rhythm in your poem. Share it with your classmates.

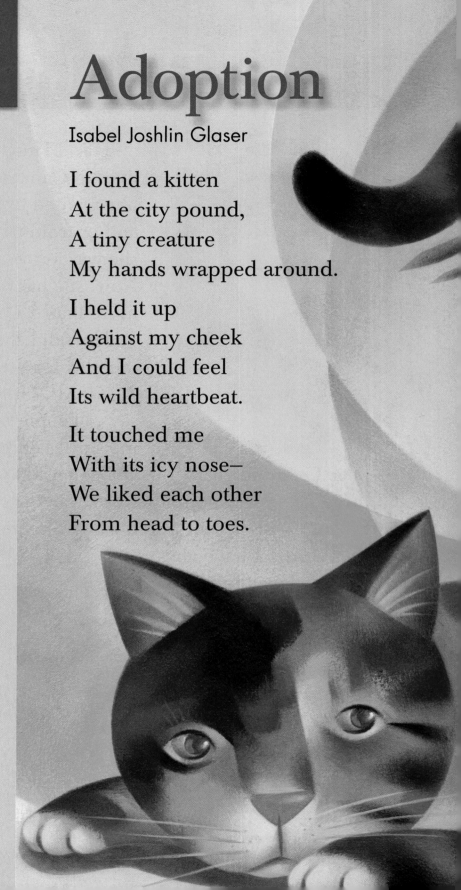

Adoption

Isabel Joshlin Glaser

I found a kitten
At the city pound,
A tiny creature
My hands wrapped around.

I held it up
Against my cheek
And I could feel
Its wild heartbeat.

It touched me
With its icy nose—
We liked each other
From head to toes.

The Stray Cat

Eve Merriam

It's just an old alley cat
that has followed us all the way home.

It hasn't a star on its forehead,
or a silky satiny coat.

No proud tiger stripes, no dainty tread,
no elegant velvet throat.

It's a splotchy, blotchy
city cat, not pretty cat,
a rough little tough little bag of old bones.

"Beauty," we shall call you.
"Beauty, come in."

Reading Across Texts

The cats in *One Dark Night* and in these two poems
are homeless. Where was each cat found?

Writing Across Texts Write a sentence
welcoming each cat to its new home.

 **Visualize** As you read, create a picture of these cats in your mind.

205

Pronouns for One and More than One

· ·

He, she, and **it** are pronouns that name only one. **We** and **they** are pronouns that name more than one.

· ·

Jonathan hears thunder. **He** races downstairs.

He is a pronoun that names one person—Jonathan.

The cat brings three kittens inside. **They** are safe from the rain.

They is a pronoun that names more than one—the cat and her kittens.

Write **Using Pronouns for One and More than One**

1. Find one sentence in the story that uses a pronoun for one. Find another sentence that uses a pronoun for more than one. Write the sentences. Underline the pronouns.

. . . .

2. Jonathan and his grandparents are kind to the cat and her kittens. Write two sentences about how you would care for the cats. Use pronouns for one and more than one.

. . . .

3. Jonathan may not be able to keep the cat and all her kittens. Write an ad that Jonathan could use to find homes for them. Use pronouns for one and more than one.

 # Plot and Theme

- A story's plot is what happens at the beginning, middle, and end of the story.

- A story's theme is the "big idea" that the author is trying to get across. Ask yourself, "What did the characters in the story learn?"

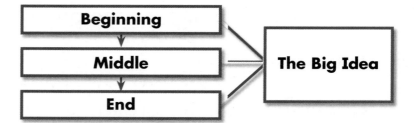

 ## Strategy: Prior Knowledge

Active readers use what they know to understand a story and its plot. Look at the title and pictures of a story. Ask, "What do I think this will be about? Do I know anything about this?"

1. Read "Trouble at the Table." Make a graphic organizer like the one above. In the final box, write the big idea of the story.

2. Choose one thing about "Trouble at the Table" that reminds you of something or someone you know. Write about it.

Trouble at the Table

Victor set the table for dinner. He did not like this job. Victor set the table for his mom, his sister Sara, and himself.

Dinner was ready. Sara ran into the room and sat in the wrong chair.

"That's my chair," Victor said.

She moved to the next chair. "That's Mom's chair," he said.

Sara sat in her own chair. Mom brought dinner to the table. Sara put her napkin on her head. Mom raised her eyebrows. Victor sighed. Sara put her napkin on her lap.

Mom put salad on the plates. Sara used a spoon to pick up the salad. Most of the lettuce fell off the spoon.

"Why don't you use your fork like us?" Victor asked.

"I am special. I didn't have to set the table," Sara told him.

Sara cut her macaroni and cheese with a knife. Then she tried to eat her pudding with a fork.

Finally Mom had had enough. "Sara," she said, "tomorrow night you can set the table." Sara sighed. Victor smiled. Mom always says stop while you're ahead.

Skill Think about the story's plot. What is happening here at the beginning of the story? You could add it to a graphic organizer.

Strategy Here you can think about the theme. Ask yourself, "Have I kept doing something even though I knew I should stop?" What is the theme of this story?

Words to Know

treat

chewing

dripping

practice

wagged

grabbed

chased

Remember

Try the strategy. Then, if you need more help, use your glossary or a dictionary.

Vocabulary Strategy
for Endings

Word Structure Sometimes when you are reading, you may come across a word you don't know. Look closely at the word. Does it have *-ed* or *-ing* at the end? The ending *-ed* or *-ing* is usually added to an action word. You may be able to use the ending to help you figure out the meaning of the word.

1. Put your finger over the *-ed* or *-ing* ending.

2. Look at the base word. (That's the word without the ending.) Do you know what the base word means?

3. Try your meaning in the sentence. Does it make sense?

Read "Rabbit Tricks." Look for words that have the *-ed* or *-ing* ending. Use the endings to help you figure out the meanings of the words.

Rabbit Tricks

"You can't teach a rabbit to do tricks," said Eric.

"Why not?" asked Lucy. "Rabbits are smart. I can train Homer. Each time he does what I want, I'll give him a treat."

Eric looked at Homer, who was chewing on a lettuce leaf. He tossed a ball across the room. "Fetch, Homer," he said. Homer sat perfectly still, the lettuce leaf dripping out of his mouth.

Lucy sighed. "Homer won't do dog tricks. He will learn to do rabbit tricks. It will just take some practice."

A week later, Lucy said to Eric, "Come and see what Homer can do." Lucy held a lettuce leaf in front of Homer and asked, "Homer, do you want this lettuce leaf?" She moved the leaf up and down. Homer wagged his head up and down. "See? Homer answered me!" Lucy said.

"He was just following you," said Eric. He grabbed the lettuce leaf and walked out of the room. Homer chased after him.

"See? Now he is playing Follow the Leader," said Lucy.

Eric gave the lettuce to Homer. "Maybe you *can* teach a rabbit to do tricks!"

What would you train Homer to do? Write about it. Use words from the Words to Know list.

211

Bad Dog, Dodger!

by Barbara Abercrombie · illustrated by Laura Ovresat

Genre

Realistic fiction means a story is possible. Look for things that could really happen to a boy and his dog.

Do the things that Dodger
does make him a bad dog?

213

Sam wanted a dog.

"If you're a good boy," said his father.

"When you can take care of it yourself," said his mother.

Sam cleaned up his room. He ate carrots and broccoli. He stopped making monster noises at night to scare Molly, his older sister. He hung up his cap after baseball practice.

On the morning of his ninth birthday, Sam found a large box waiting for him. Inside was a puppy. He was black and soft and had big feet. Sam named him Dodger.

The whole family loved Dodger. Dodger licked their faces and curled up on their laps. He nibbled their shoelaces.

215

One day Dodger knocked the trash
all over the kitchen floor.

"Bad dog, Dodger!" said Sam.

Dodger wagged his tail and wanted
to play, but Sam was already late for
baseball practice.

When Molly was taking a bath one night, Dodger jumped into the tub with her. She started to scream. Dodger jumped out and raced through the house dripping water.

Sam and his father chased him with towels.

"Bad dog, Dodger!" yelled Sam.

"He's not bad," said his father. "He just wants to play."

One morning Sam found Dodger chewing his baseball cap. There was a big hole in it. Sam was so mad he almost cried.

They were eating dinner when Dodger pulled down the living room curtains. He wore them into the kitchen. He looked like a bride.

"I've had it," said Sam's mother. "This dog has to live outside."

The next day Dodger jumped over the fence and followed Sam to school and into his classroom.

He knocked over the hamster cage. He ate the cover off a spelling book. Sam's mother had to leave work to take Dodger home.

Saturday was Sam's first Little League game. He was up at bat when Dodger came flying onto the field.

The umpire yelled, "Time out!"

The other team booed.

The coach yelled, "Get that dog!"

219

Dodger grabbed the bat and ran around the field with it. The umpire and the coach ran after him. Sam had to leave the game to take Dodger home.

"We can't go on like this," said Sam's mother. "Maybe Dodger would be better off with somebody who had more time."

Sam knew his mother was right. Dodger needed more attention.

Sam went out and sat in the doghouse with Dodger. "I love you, Dodger." Dodger's tail thumped up and down. "But you need to practice being a good dog."

Suddenly Sam had an idea.

That night he set his alarm to go off half an hour early.

The family was still asleep when Sam got up
the next morning. In the kitchen he filled his pockets
with dog treats.

"Wake up, Dodger!"

Sam pitched a ball to Dodger. Dodger caught it.
"Good dog, Dodger!"

Sam waved a treat in the air. "Come!"

Dodger pranced around the yard with the ball
in his mouth. "This is training, not a game!" yelled Sam.

Finally Dodger set the ball down at Sam's feet. Sam
gave him a treat and said, "Good dog, Dodger!"

"Dodger's in spring training," Sam told his parents at breakfast.

Sam pitched balls to Dodger every morning. "Come, Dodger!" he'd shout, waving a treat when Dodger caught the ball.

"Sit!" And Sam would push Dodger's bottom down to show him what sit meant. "Stay!"

After a month of training, Sam decided Dodger was ready to come to a baseball game.

Dodger sat in the bleachers next to Sam's parents.

In the ninth inning, Sam was up at bat with two strikes and the bases loaded. The score was tied. The pitcher wound up to pitch. Everybody held their breath. Sam gripped the bat and hit a fly ball over the bleachers.

"Foul!" yelled the umpire.

Suddenly a flash of black fur leaped into the air to catch the ball.

Oh, no, thought Sam as the umpire called "Time out!" and the game stopped.

"That crazy dog again!" cried the coach. The other team was laughing. Sam's mother was shaking her head.

223

Dodger trotted toward Sam with the ball in his mouth. He dropped it at Sam's feet.

"Good dog," said Sam.

He walked Dodger to the dugout. "Sit." Dodger sat.

All the spectators grew very quiet. The other team stopped laughing.

"Stay," said Sam.

Dodger stayed.

Sam hit the next pitch right over the fence for a home run. He ran to first, second, third base.

As he reached home plate, he called, "Come, Dodger!" and everyone clapped. Even the coach.

After the game, the team had their picture taken. Dodger was in the front row and got to wear Sam's baseball cap.

Reader Response

Open for Discussion Sam says, "Bad dog!" Later, Sam says, "Good dog!" If Dodger could talk, what would he say about the two sentences?

1. The author uses lively verbs to show Dodger's actions. Find seven lively verbs for Dodger's actions. Read them aloud to make them sound like actions.

2. How did Sam take responsibility for Dodger's behavior?

3. What do you know or what have you read about training a pet? How did that help you understand Sam and Dodger?

4. Make a list of action verbs from the story and the Words to Know list. Next to each verb write a word that completes the action in the story. Examples: *licked—faces* and *nibbled—shoelaces.*

Look Back and Write Find three commands that Sam uses. List them and write why each command is important for a dog like Dodger to learn to obey.

Meet the Author

Barbara Abercrombie

Read two more books by Barbara Abercrombie.

Barbara Abercrombie began writing stories when she was six years old. She likes to write about pets. "When my children were growing up, we had dogs. Our favorite was a Newfoundland named Jennifer. She looked like a large black bear and was often naughty, but we loved her very much. We let her sleep in our beds with the cats." Ms. Abercrombie has two cats now, Stuart Little and Charlotte Webb. Two of her books are about cats.

Charlie Anderson

Michael and the Cats

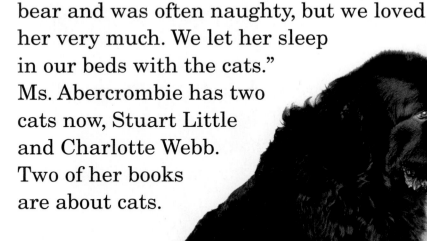

227

How-to Article

Genre

- **How-to articles explain how to do something one step at a time.**

Text Features

- **This how-to article has numbered steps that give examples to help you train your puppy.**

- **Photos also help explain what to do.**

Link to Science

Use the library or the Internet to find out more about training other types of animals. Make a poster with steps to show how to do it. Tell the class about your poster.

How to Train Your Puppy

by L.B. Coombs

Have you ever tried to make a puppy behave? Training a puppy means making it do the same thing over and over again. You can train a puppy, or most any pet, too. Here's how.

- Begin training when your puppy is very young.

- Teach your puppy to do only one new thing at a time.

- Pick one word as the command for each new thing you want the puppy to learn, but don't repeat the command too many times.

The words and pictures that follow will help you train your puppy.

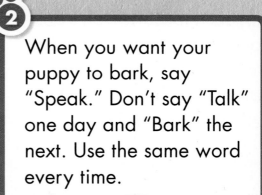

1 First, let your puppy get to know you. Let him sniff your hand. He will learn to know you by your smell.

2 When you want your puppy to bark, say "Speak." Don't say "Talk" one day and "Bark" the next. Use the same word every time.

Speak!

Prior Knowledge What do you know about dogs that helps you understand this?

3

Do not yell at your puppy. This might scare him. Say "No" firmly and in a deep voice. If "No" is the word you want him to remember, use it all the time. Do not say "Stop" or "Don't" when you mean "No."

4

Train your puppy to walk on a leash. Hold your end of the leash loosely. Don't pull your puppy with the leash. Play with your puppy while he is on the leash. It will help him get used to it.

5

After your puppy has done what you ask, tell him he did a good job. Reward him with a treat. Hug and pat your puppy. Training will be fun for both of you.

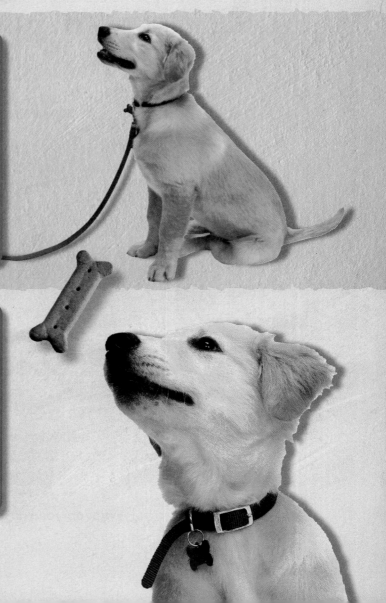

You might want to teach your puppy to sit and stay. When your puppy is standing, gently push his bottom to the ground and say "Sit." After your puppy sits, say "Stay." When your puppy sits and stays for a while, praise him and give him a treat.

It takes time to train a puppy. But if you choose to do it, this training time can be good for both of you. You and your puppy will build a special friendship.

Reading Across Texts

In *Bad Dog, Dodger,* which rules from "How to Train Your Puppy" did Sam use?

Writing Across Texts
Choose another rule and write a note to Sam explaining why he should follow this rule with Dodger.

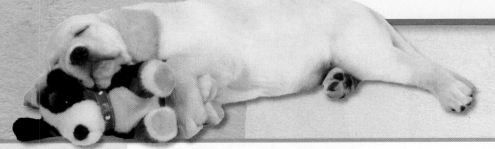

Prior Knowledge How does what you already know help you understand this?

Using I and Me

The pronouns **I** and **me** take the place of your name. Use **I** as the subject of a sentence. Use **me** after an action verb. Always write **I** with a capital letter. When you talk about yourself and another person, name yourself last.

I read a story to Al about a funny dog. The story made Al and **me** laugh.

The pronouns **I** and **me** take the place of your name.

232

Write Using I and Me

1. Turn to page 220. Find the sentence that tells how Sam feels about Dodger. Write the sentence and underline the pronouns.

2. Think about what you would do to help a pet who gets into trouble. Write two or three sentences. Use the pronouns *I* and *me*.

3. Pretend you are Sam. Write a note to convince your parents that you can help Dodger. Use the pronouns *I* and *me* instead of your name.

Skill

Author's Purpose

An author has reasons for writing.
The author may want

- to share important information.
- to explain something.
- to tell an interesting story.

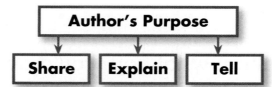

Author's Purpose		
Share	Explain	Tell

Strategy

Strategy: Ask Questions

Good readers ask themselves questions before, during, and after they read. This will help you understand what you read. This will also help you decide what the author's purpose is.

Write

1. Read "What to Do?" Think about why the author wrote the story. Use the chart above to help you.

2. As you read, write some questions to ask yourself.

What to Do?

Janet and Erica met after school like they always did. "What do you want to do?" Erica asked. "I really, really want to go to the playground."

Janet said, "I really, really don't. I want to work on our clubhouse."

Erica was surprised. They always wanted to do the same thing. "How about we solve a mystery?" Erica asked.

"No. How about we bother your brother?" Janet replied.

The two friends looked at each other. "Maybe we won't play today," Janet said.

Erica really wanted to play with Janet. She had a thought. "How about today we do what you want to do, and tomorrow we do what I want to do?"

Janet smiled and said, "That's what I would really, really like to do."

Strategy Here's a good spot to ask yourself a question. What is happening between these two characters?

Skill Now that you have read the story, ask yourself, What idea did the author want me to understand?

235

Words to Know

adventure

wondered

exploring

climbed

clubhouse

greatest

truest

Try the strategy. Then, if you need more help, use your glossary or a dictionary.

Vocabulary Strategy
for Endings

Word Structure As you read, you may see a word you don't know. What can you do? Look at the end of the word. The ending *-est* is often added to a describing word when comparing three or more things, as in *smallest*. You may be able to use the ending to help you figure out the meaning of the word.

1. Put your finger over the ending.

2. Look at the base word. Do you know what the base word means?

3. Try your meaning in the sentence. Does it make sense?

Read "Boris and Cloris." Look for words that have the *-est* ending. Use the ending to help you figure out the meanings.

Boris and Cloris

Boris was bored. All he did was eat cheese and scamper across the floor. Boris longed for adventure, something exciting.

At the far end of the backyard was a small building. Boris wondered what was in it.

He asked his friend Cloris to go exploring with him, but she refused. So Boris went alone.

When he got to the building, Boris climbed through a hole in a board. Two girls were sitting on the floor, talking.

"Who will we allow in our clubhouse?" asked one girl.

"Only our best friends, the greatest and the truest of our friends," said the other girl. "But, look! There's a mouse in our clubhouse!"

The two girls jumped up and tried to catch Boris. He raced for the hole, but where was it? "Over here, Boris," Cloris squeaked. Boris jumped through the hole, and they dashed across the backyard.

When they were safe at home, Boris said to Cloris, "Thank you for coming after me. You are the greatest and truest friend." And he never longed for adventure again.

Write

What do you like to do with a friend? Write about your friend. Use the Words to Know list.

237

Horace and Morris

Fantasies are make-believe stories because they couldn't really happen. What makes this story a fantasy?

but mostly Dolores

by James Howe

illustrated by Amy Walrod

Will Horace, Morris, and Dolores remain very good friends?

Horace and Morris but mostly Dolores
loved adventure. They sailed the seven sewers.

They climbed Mount Ever-Rust. They dared to go where
no mouse had gone before.

Horace and Morris but mostly Dolores never said,
"This is something we shouldn't do."

They said, "This is something we've *got* to do!"
And so there was almost nothing they didn't do.

243

Horace and Morris and Dolores were friends—the greatest of friends, the truest of friends, the now-and-forever-I'm-yours sort of friends. And then one day . . . Horace and Morris had a decision to make.

They didn't want to do anything without Dolores, but as Horace pointed out, "A boy mouse must do what a boy mouse must do."

"Bet you can't say *that* three times real fast," Dolores said with a smile.

Horace and Morris didn't even try. They didn't even smile.
"Good-bye, Dolores," they said.

What kind of place doesn't allow girls? Dolores wondered
as she watched her friends step through the door of the
Mega-Mice clubhouse.

Downhearted, Dolores went on her way—alone. It wasn't long before . . . Dolores had a decision to make.

She didn't really want to do anything without Horace and Morris, but she figured a girl mouse must do what a girl mouse must do. (She said this aloud three times real fast just to prove that she could.)

A GIRL MOUSE MUST DO WHAT A GIRL MOUSE MUST DO.

I'll bet Horace and Morris couldn't do that, she thought. But she wasn't smiling as she stepped through the door of the Cheese Puffs clubhouse.

Day after day, Dolores went to the Cheese Puffs. Day after day, Horace and Morris went to Mega-Mice.

They missed playing with each other, but as they said . . . "A girl mouse must do what a girl mouse must do." "A boy mouse must do what a boy mouse must do."

Horace and Morris and even Dolores were sure their friendship would never be the same. But then one day . . . Dolores made a different decision.

247

"I'm bored," she announced.

The other girls stared.

"Anybody here want to build a fort? How about a Roque-fort?"

The other girls booed.

"Okay, forget the cheese. I'm sick of making things out of cheese anyway. Let's go exploring."

The other girls gasped.

"Phooey!" said Dolores. "I quit!"

"If you quit, then I quit too!" a small voice said from the back of the room.

Outside Dolores introduced herself. "I'm Dolores."

"I'm Chloris," said the girl.

250

"Now where can we go to have some *real* fun around here?" Dolores thought and thought. "I've got it!" she said at last.

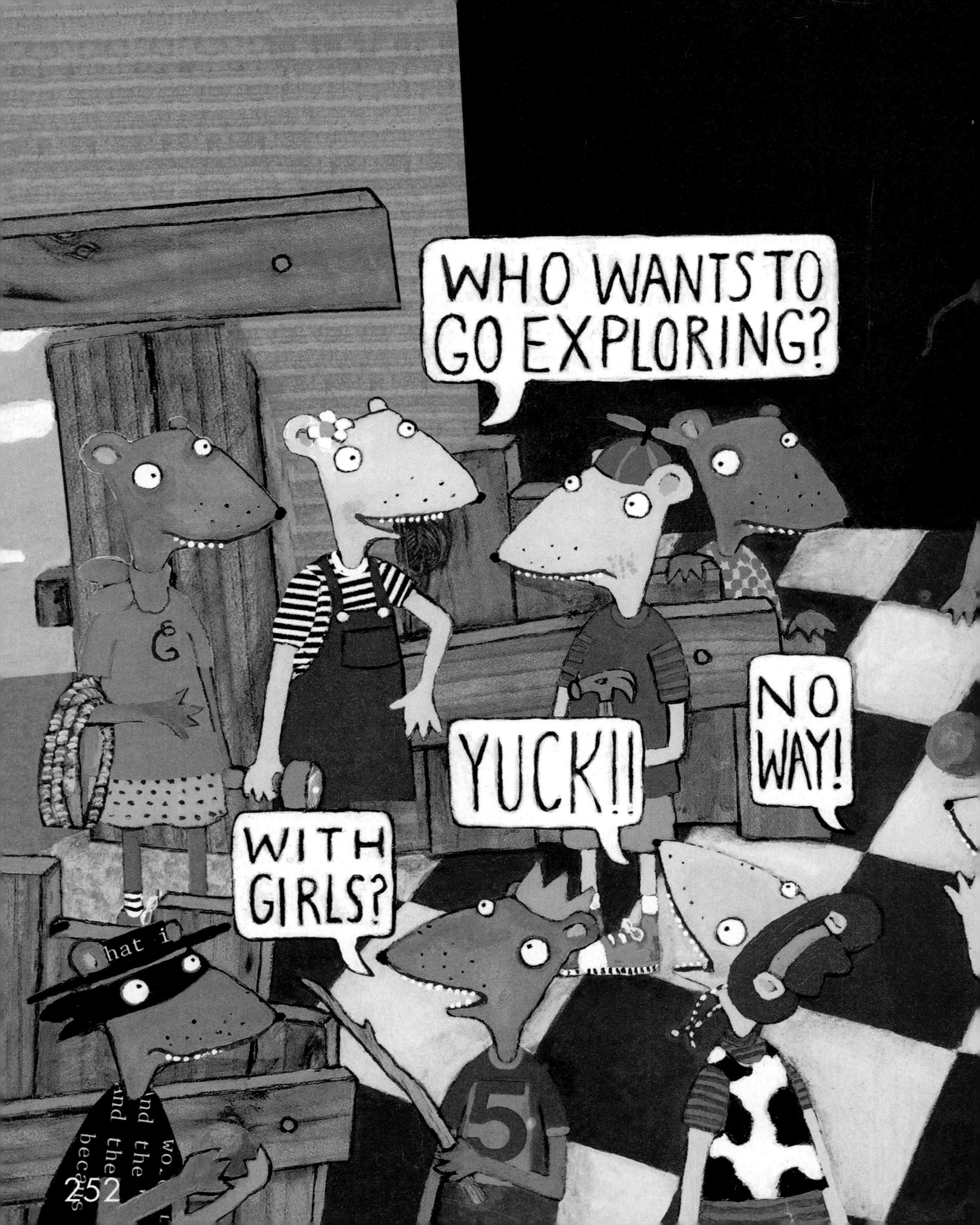
WHO WANTS TO GO EXPLORING?
WITH GIRLS?
YUCK!!
NO WAY!

253

The five friends spent the rest of the day
exploring, Chloris and Boris and Horace and
Morris . . . but mostly Dolores . . .

And the next day they built a clubhouse of their own.

Reader Response

Open for Discussion Imagine that you are Horace or Morris or Dolores. Tell how things changed for you in this story.

1. The three friends had adventures. What examples does the author give you to help you know about these adventures?

2. This is a funny, entertaining story. What other message do you think the author might be trying to give you?

3. Did anything in this story confuse you? What questions did you ask yourself as you read?

4. Write an ad to get members to join the Frisky Whisker Club. Use words from the Words to Know list.

Look Back and Write Find two sentences in the story that would be hard to say three times! Now write two new hard-to-say sentences for the Frisky Whisker Club.

Meet the Author and Illustrator
James Howe and Amy Walrod

Read two more books by James Howe or illustrated by Amy Walrod.

James Howe loves words. He has enjoyed playing with words ever since he was a boy when he began writing stories and plays. Mr. Howe has written more than 70 books about funny characters including Bunnicula and Pinky and Rex. He thinks that the best way to be a good writer is to read—and write, write, write!

Horace and Morris Join the Chorus (but what about Dolores?)

Amy Walrod's first picture book was *Horace and Morris but mostly Dolores*. Ms. Walrod likes to collect things. She collects toys, lunch boxes, cupcake ornaments, sparkly things, and stuff she finds on the ground. Can you find any of the things she likes to collect in her pictures?

The Little Red Hen Makes a Pizza

257

Social Studies in Reading

Newspaper Article

Genre

- Newspaper articles may cover news about the city, the nation, or the world.

Text Features

- Newspaper articles usually have catchy headlines that grab the reader's attention.

- Photographs and captions give more information.

- Quotes from a real person help the reader know that the article is true and factual.

Link to Social Studies

Find out more about famous soccer players. Make a poster to report your findings.

Good Kicking

by Rich Richardson
Staff Writer

From spring to fall, you can hear the whoops and hollers of happy children. What's happening? They are playing one of the fastest growing sports around—soccer!

Soccer is played in almost every country in the world. Boys and girls of all ages love this fast-moving sport. Soccer is played in schools and parks across America. Some towns have put together teams of children that play each other.

The small towns around Chicago have some of the best young soccer players. Some children begin playing on teams when they are as young as four or five.

These players chase down the ball.

Good kicking means good foot work.

Ask Questions   What question do you have for the writer?

"We want everyone to have fun," says Coach Kay of the Goalers, a team of seven-year-olds. "We have a mixed team of boys and girls. They learn to play together as they learn the rules of the game. Most importantly, they learn what it means to be a part of a team."

Anyone who has ever played a team sport knows that each team member is important. Team members have a responsibility to do the best job they can. If each team member does his or her job right, the team has fun and everybody wins.

"It's always nice to win," Coach Kay states.

Trident players chase down the ball for their team.

Two members of the Scooters congratulate each other.

Author's Purpose   Why did the writer write this article?

Coach Kay and members of the Goalers relax before a game. "Being part of a team is more than just winning," Coach Kay says.

"But it's also important that children have fun. Being part of a team is more than just winning. It's learning your role as a team member and knowing your responsibility to your fellow teammates. If we all work together, everybody wins."

Coach Kay should know. Her team, the Goalers, has not lost a game all season. The laughter and smiles on the children's faces also show that they have fun.

Reading Across Texts
Do you think Dolores would have liked playing soccer for the Goalers and Coach Kay?

Writing Across Texts
Write a short paragraph telling why you feel as you do.

Different Kinds of Pronouns

The pronouns **I, he, she, we,** and **they** are used as subjects of sentences. The pronouns **me, him, her, us,** and **them** are used after action verbs. The pronouns **you** and **it** can be used anywhere in a sentence.

Dolores loved adventure. **She** went where no mouse had gone before.

The pronoun **she** is the subject of the sentence.

There stood Mount Ever-Rust. Dolores climbed **it** quickly.

The pronoun **it** is used after the action verb *climbed.*

Write Using Different Kinds of Pronouns

1. Find a sentence in the story with a pronoun used as the subject of the sentence. Write the sentence. Underline the pronoun.

· ·

2. Dolores worked out a problem she had with her friends. Write two sentences that tell how you have worked out a problem. Use different kinds of pronouns.

· ·

3. Write two or three sentences that tell friends why they should read *Horace and Morris but mostly Dolores.* Use pronouns as subjects and after action verbs.

Comprehension

Skill
Realism
and Fantasy

Strategy
Monitor
and Fix Up

Skill

Realism and Fantasy

- A realistic story tells about things that could happen.

- A fantasy is a story that tells about things that could never happen.

What's Real	What's Not

Strategy

Strategy: Monitor and Fix Up

Active readers make sure they understand what they are reading. If during reading you do not understand what's happening, go back and reread part of the story. Did you find something that makes the story clearer? Then read on.

1. Read "One Fine Afternoon." Make a graphic organizer like the one above. Write what is real and what is not.

2. As you read, write questions about what is happening in the story. Answer those questions by rereading or by reading on.

One Fine Afternoon

What a boring day! Alex's good friend was sick. His other good friend had gone away on a trip. Alex missed his friends. He went into his room and closed the door.

His dog Rags sat on the rug and thumped his tail. Dancer the cat watched Alex sit on his bed and sigh.

"Bored?" Rags asked.

"What?" Alex's eyes grew big as he looked at his dog.

Strategy Ask yourself, "Do I understand what's going on?" If not, read on. See if things begin to make sense.

"He asked if you are bored?" Dancer repeated.

"You—you can talk!"

"Of course," Rags said.

"Always could," Dancer told Alex. "You just never listened."

Alex was a little surprised to hear his pets speak like people. He asked softly, "So, you think maybe we could all play?"

"Thought you'd never ask!" Rags said and carried a ball over to Alex. "Let's play!"

Skill Is this real? Can pets really talk to you like people do?

signmaker

townspeople

afternoon

blame

important

idea

Remember

Try the strategy. Then, if you need more help, use your glossary or a dictionary.

Vocabulary Strategy
for Compound Words

Word Structure When you are reading, you may come to a long word. Do you see two small words in it? Then it could be a compound word. You may be able to use the two small words to help you figure out the meaning of the compound word. For example, a *mailbox* is a box in which we put our mail.

1. Divide the compound word into its two small words.

2. Think of the meaning of each small word. Put the two meanings together. Does this help you understand the meaning of the compound word?

3. Try the meaning in the sentence. Does it make sense?

Read "Sigmund's Sign." Use the meanings of the small words in a compound word to help you understand its meaning.

Sigmund's Sign

Sigmund was a signmaker. Every shop, every building, and every house in the town had one of Sigmund's signs. The signs told what was sold in the shop (Toys) or who worked in the building (Police) or who lived in the house (The Guntersons). The signs were very useful. They helped the townspeople find their way around the town.

But Sigmund thought that signs could do much more than that. One afternoon a large sign appeared in the town square. It said, "Don't blame them." People stopped to read the sign. Then they talked to one another about the sign. They wondered what the sign meant. They thought about their own actions. Had they blamed someone? Had they been unfair?

Sitting in his signmaking shop, Sigmund smiled. He knew that a sign could do more than help people find their way around. A sign could make people think about an important idea. Sigmund began to paint another large sign.

Write

What sign do you think Sigmund painted next? Write about it. Use words from the Words to Know list.

Humorous fiction is a funny story about imaginary people and events. Look for the funny things that happen in this story.

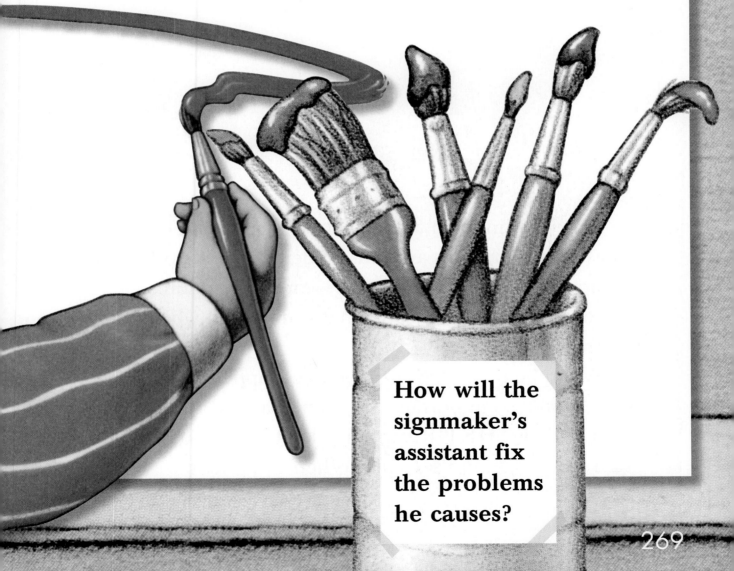

THE SIGNMAKER's ASSISTANT

by Tedd Arnold

How will the
signmaker's
assistant fix
the problems
he causes?

Everyone in town agreed. The old signmaker did the finest work for miles around. Under his brush, ordinary letters became beautiful words—words of wisdom, words of warning, or words that simply said which door to use.

When he painted STOP, people stopped because the sign looked so important. When he painted PLEASE KEEP OFF THE GRASS, they kept off because the sign was polite and sensible. When he painted

GOOD FOOD, they just naturally became hungry.

People thanked the signmaker and paid him well. But the kind old man never failed to say, "I couldn't have done it without Norman's help."

Norman was the signmaker's assistant. Each day after school he cut wood, mixed colors, and painted simple signs.

"Soon I will have a shop of my own," said Norman.

"Perhaps," answered the signmaker, "but not before you clean these brushes."

One day, after his work was done, Norman stood at a window over the sign shop and watched people. They stopped at the STOP sign. They entered at the ENTER sign. They ate under the GOOD FOOD sign.

"They do whatever the signs say!" said Norman to himself. "I wonder. . ." He crept into the shop while the signmaker napped. With brush and board he painted a sign of his own.

Early the next morning he put up the sign, then ran back to his window to watch.

"No school?" muttered the principal. "How could I forget such a thing?"

"No one informed me," said the teacher.

"Hooray!" cheered the children, and everyone went home.

"This is great!" cried Norman. He looked around town for another idea. "Oh," he said at last, "there is something I have always wanted to do."

The following day Norman jumped from the top of the fountain in the park. As he swam, he thought to himself, *I can do lots of things with signs.* Ideas filled his head.

That afternoon when Norman went to work, the signmaker said, "I must drive to the next town and paint a large sign on a storefront. I'll return tomorrow evening, so please lock up the shop tonight."

As soon as the signmaker was gone, Norman started making signs. He painted for hours and hours and hours.

In the morning people discovered new signs all around town.

275

Norman watched it all
and laughed until tears came
to his eyes. But soon he saw
people becoming angry.

277

"The signmaker is playing tricks," they shouted. "He has made fools of us!"

The teacher tore down the NO SCHOOL TODAY sign. Suddenly people were tearing down all the signs—not just the new ones but every sign the signmaker had ever painted.

Then the real trouble started. Without store signs, shoppers became confused. Without stop signs, drivers didn't know when to stop. Without street signs, firemen became lost.

In the evening when the signmaker returned
from his work in the next town, he knew nothing of
Norman's tricks. An angry crowd of people met him at
the back door of his shop and chased him into
the woods.

As Norman watched, he suddenly realized that
without signs and without the signmaker, the town was
in danger.

"It's all my fault!" cried Norman, but no one
was listening.

DON'T BLAME THE SIGNMAKER
I TRICKED YOU AND I'M SORRY. —Norman

Late that night the signmaker returned and saw a light on in his shop. Norman was feverishly painting.

While the town slept and the signmaker watched, Norman put up stop signs, shop signs, street signs, danger signs, and welcome signs; in and out signs, large and small signs, new and beautiful signs. He returned all his presents and cleared away the garbage at the grocery store. It was morning when he finished putting up his last sign for the entire town to see.

Then Norman packed his things and locked up the shop. But as he turned to go, he discovered the signmaker and all the townspeople gathered at the door.

"I know you're angry with me for what I did," said Norman with downcast eyes, "so I'm leaving."

"Oh, we were angry all right!" answered the school principal. "But we were also fools for obeying signs without thinking."

"You told us you are sorry," said the signmaker, "and you fixed your mistakes. So stay and work hard. One day this shop may be yours."

"Perhaps," answered Norman, hugging the old man, "but not before I finish cleaning those brushes."

Reader Response

Open for Discussion Suppose Norman asks to come and work in your community. What will you say to him?

1. The author could have written, "Signs are important!" Instead, he showed you that this is true. How did he do that?

2. Why couldn't this story happen in real life?

3. Think about the signs you see every day. How does this help you know that *The Signmaker's Assistant* is a make-believe story?

4. Here are some compound words from the story: *signmaker, townspeople, afternoon, storefront, without.* Use one of the two small words in each to make a new compound word.

Look Back and Write On page 273, Norman says, "They do whatever the signs say!" Then he says, "I wonder. . . ." Write what Norman wondered and what he later found out.

Tedd Arnold

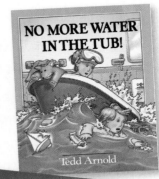

No More Water in the Tub

The library is one of Tedd Arnold's favorite places to go. He gets ideas there. Once he rode a bus through a town and noticed all the store signs. The signs were nice, and he thought about the person who painted them. The signmaker told people where to go. He controlled what the neighborhood looked like. Mr. Arnold said, "I began to wonder how else a signmaker might have control. Of course, I started thinking of silly signs that could control people and make them do goofy things. That's how the story got started!"

Tracks

285

Evaluating Sources

Genre

- You can find information fast on the Internet.

- You need to decide what is good information and what's not.

Text Features

- The addresses of Web sites you can count on often end in *.gov*, *.edu*, or *.org*.

- Web sites that end in *.com* may also be useful, but you must check them carefully. The description with the address can help you choose.

Link to Social Studies

- Find out about a volunteer group in your area. Report about it.

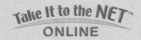
Helping Hand

The signmaker learned about being responsible. You can do an Internet search to find out how you can help your neighbors. Use a search engine and type in the keyword *volunteer*. Here are two topics you might find listed. Which one would tell you about volunteer work? To choose, look carefully at both the source and the description.

This is a .com Web site. A .com site often sells things. It may or may not be a good source.

File   Edit   View   Favorites   Tools   Help

http://www.url.here

Show Your Colors. T-shirts, bumper stickers, decals, and other items can show your loyalty to a group that you support.

Organizations Started by Kids. Think you're too young to start your own organization? Hmm . . . maybe you'll change your mind after seeing what these kids have done.

This is a .org Web site. A .org site is usually a good source.

(C) **Monitor and Fix Up**   If necessary, reread what you've read.

The link Organizations Started by Kids looks good to you. When you click on it, you get a list of other links. Here are some of them:

File   Edit   View   Favorites   Tools   Help

http://www.url.here

Organizations Started by Kids

Care Bags Foundation Annie Wignall, eleven years old

Grandma's Gifts Emily Douglas, nine years old

Kids For A Clean Environment (F.A.C.E.) Melissa Poe, nine years old

Kids Saving the Rain Forest Janine Licare Andrews and Aislin Livingstone, nine years old

Pennies to Protect Police Dogs Stacey Hillman, eleven years old

You may want to know more about these volunteer organizations. You decide to explore some of these links by clicking on them.

File   Edit   View   Favorites   Tools   Help

http://www.url.here

Kids For A Clean Environment (F.A.C.E.)

Kids F.A.C.E. is an environmental group. Kids from around the world belong to it. It was started in 1989 by nine-year-old Melissa Poe of Nashville, Tennessee. The club provides a way for children to protect nature. The club connects them with other children who share their concerns about environmental issues. Kids F.A.C.E. currently has 300,000 members.

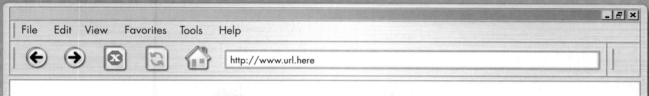

Pennies to Protect Police Dogs

Eleven-year-old Stacey Hillman started Pennies to Protect Police Dogs. She had read about police dogs and their dangerous jobs. One police dog had been shot on the job. The article mentioned that there were bulletproof vests for police dogs, but the vests cost a lot. Over the years, Pennies to Protect Police Dogs has raised more than $100,000. The group has outfitted over 158 K-9 dogs with bulletproof vests.

After reading about both of these groups, you can decide which one might be best for you.

Reading Across Texts

The signmaker's assistant realizes that he has a responsibility to his neighbors. Kid volunteers also help their neighbors. Which group do you think the signmaker's assistant might join?

Writing Across Texts Write a short paragraph explaining how the signmaker's assistant might help his neighbors.

 Monitor and Fix Up   Confused? Remember to reread.

Contractions

A **contraction** is a short way to put two words together. An **apostrophe (')** takes the place of one or more letters. Contractions can combine a pronoun and a word, such as *will*, *are*, or *is*.

Soon **I'll** have a shop of my own.

The contraction **I'll** is a short way of writing **I will**.

Many contractions are formed with verbs and the word *not*.

Please **don't** throw away that sign.

The contraction **don't** is a short way of writing **do not**.

Write Using Contractions

1. Find a sentence in the story with a contraction. Write the sentence and underline the contraction. Write the two words the contraction replaces.

2. Norman was sad about what he did. He used contractions when he said *"I'm* sorry" and *"It's* all my fault!" Write about something you did that made you happy. Use some contractions.

3. Write a letter to persuade a friend to visit you during the summer. Use contractions.

Job Chart

connect to **SOCIAL STUDIES**

In Unit 5, you read about people who are responsible in different ways. Each person in a certain role or job needs to have special skills and training to do a job well. Make a chart. Show each job or role you read about. List a few important skills for doing the job well.

Job	Skill
Firefighter	Strong

What does it mean to be responsible?

Responsibility Book

connect to
WRITING

Do you help around the house? Maybe you do something special for a neighbor or take care of a pet. Think about one way you know how to be responsible. Make a book to teach someone else how to do this. Put a drawing on each page. Write a sentence or two for each picture.

I help feed the neighbor's cat when he is away.

Great Helpers

connect to
SOCIAL
STUDIES

Tell a partner about different jobs you might like to do when you are grown up. Talk about ways that you could help others and be responsible as you do each job.

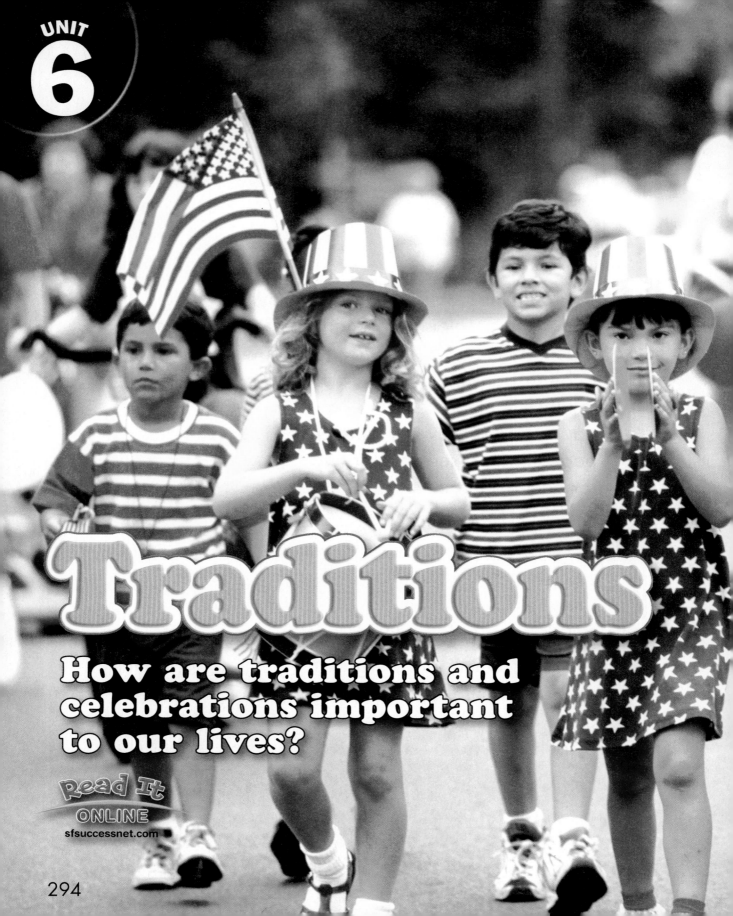

Traditions

How are traditions and celebrations important to our lives?

Read It
ONLINE
sfsuccessnet.com

connect to
SOCIAL STUDIES

Just Like Josh Gibson

Grandmama shares the tradition of American baseball.

Realistic Fiction

connect to
SOCIAL STUDIES

Red, White, and Blue: The Story of the American Flag

Our nation's flag is a traditional symbol.

Narrative Nonfiction

connect to
SOCIAL STUDIES

A Birthday Basket for Tía

Birthdays are an important family tradition.

Realistic Fiction

connect to
SOCIAL STUDIES

Cowboys

Cowboys are an American tradition.

Narrative Nonfiction

connect to
SOCIAL STUDIES

Jingle Dancer

Jenna participates in a Native American tradition.

Realistic Fiction

Comprehension

Skill
Compare
and Contrast

Strategy
Visualize

Compare
and Contrast

- When you compare and contrast, you see how things are alike and different.

- You can compare and contrast things you read about with things you already know.

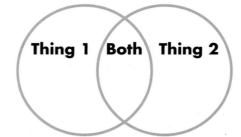

Thing 1 | Both | Thing 2

Strategy: Visualize

As good readers read, they picture in their minds how something looks, sounds, feels, tastes, or smells. Picturing can help you compare what you are reading with what you already know.

1. Read "Pepper Davis, Play Ball!" Make a diagram like the one above. Fill in the diagram to compare and contrast baseball today and long ago.

2. Then use your diagram to write a paragraph that compares and contrasts a player like Pepper Davis with a baseball player today.

Pepper Davis, Play Ball!

ADMIT ONE

Pepper Davis loved to play baseball with her brother, Joe. Pepper had a good arm. In fact, she played better than Joe.

It was wartime. Many men were away fighting the war. That's when the All American Girls Baseball League began. Pepper worked hard to make a team. She became a catcher.

The girl baseball players played games almost every day during the summer. They rode a bus from town to town. They threw, hit, and ran well. The best players made 85 dollars a week.

The girls played in short skirts. They also had to act like young ladies. They took beauty lessons to learn proper behavior.

Pepper loved to win. She played baseball for ten years. Today she is in the Baseball Hall of Fame.

Skill This is a good place to compare these facts with what you know about baseball players today.

Strategy Try visualizing how the girl baseball players looked.

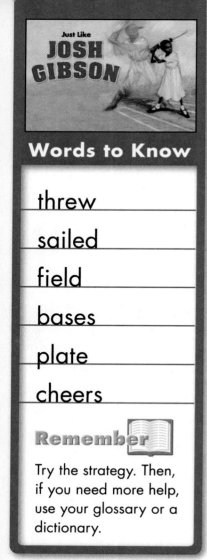

threw

sailed

field

bases

plate

cheers

Remember

Try the strategy. Then, if you need more help, use your glossary or a dictionary.

Vocabulary Strategy
for Multiple-Meaning Words

Context Clues What do you do when you come to a word you know, but the meaning of the word doesn't fit in the sentence? You should think to yourself that the word may have more than one meaning. For example, *bat* means "a stick used to hit a ball." *Bat* also means "a flying animal."

1. Try the meaning you know. Does it make sense in the sentence?

2. If it doesn't, the word may have another meaning. Read on and look at the nearby words. Can you figure out another meaning?

3. Try the new meaning in the sentence. Does it make sense?

Read "Tigers Over Lions." Look for words that can have more than one meaning. Remember to use nearby words to figure out a new meaning.

Tigers Over Lions

The fifth-place Terryville Tigers played the sixth-place Lincoln Lions last night. The game promised to be an even contest. Tiger pitcher Mike Petrov has won nine games so far. Lion pitcher Kurt Geiger has won 10. Both teams have good hitters. But Petrov had a great night. He threw a perfect game. Geiger was perfect too. Well . . . almost. For eight and one-half innings, Petrov and Geiger did not give up a hit. Batter after batter went down swinging, popped up, or flied out.

In the bottom of the ninth, the Tigers' last batter was Darrell Swann. He looked at a ball and took two strikes. Then Geiger threw a ball hard and outside, and Swann hit it. The ball sailed into the far corner of right field. Swann raced around the bases. He slid across home plate just before the tag. The umpire yelled, "Safe!" The cheers of the crowd said it all. The Tigers won the game 1–0.

Write

Write about an exciting game you have played. Use as many words from the Words to Know list as you can.

299

Just Like

JOSH GIBSON

by Angela Johnson
illustrated by Beth Peck

Can a girl really hit a baseball just like Josh Gibson?

Grandmama says there's
nothing like baseball.
The story goes. . . .

Josh Gibson once hit a
baseball in Pittsburgh so hard
that it didn't come down.

The next day he was playing in Philadelphia, and the ball dropped out of the sky, right into a fielder's glove. The umpire pointed at Josh and said, "You're out yesterday in Pittsburgh!"

Grandmama says her papa showed up on that same day, the day she was born, with a Louisville slugger and a smile. He said his new baby would make baseballs fly, just like Josh Gibson.

So Grandmama's papa threw balls to his baby girl in the early morning dew. Those summer days were like magic as the balls sailed away, sailed away, gone.

But girls in the forties didn't play baseball. They weren't supposed to take the field with the boys or have batting dreams.

So even when Grandmama got bigger, she still had to stand outside the fence and watch her cousin Danny and the Maple Grove All-Stars batting away.

But every now and again, when the team was just practicing, they'd let Grandmama play too. Then Grandmama would step up to the plate, hit the ball, and watch it soar.

Grandmama says Danny would imagine he was playing with the Dodgers. But she was always Josh Gibson, playing for the Grays, wearing the team colors and hitting away.

Grandmama says she would play all day, with everybody saying she could do it all, hit, throw, and fly round the bases. "But too bad she's a girl. . . ."
Too bad she's a girl. . . .

Until . . . two days,
hot days after the Fourth
of July, Danny hurt his
arm sliding into second,
and there were only
eight All-Stars.

That afternoon the
team looked to
Grandmama—
pink dress with
a white bow, and
Danny's baseball shoes.

And Grandmama
says as she went
to the plate she
remembered . . .

baseball has always been
early morning dew and
sunlight, hitting balls with
her papa, and standing
behind the fence,
watching the boys play.

309

The story goes . . .
Grandmama hit the ball a mile
that day, caught anything that
was thrown, and did everything
else—just like Josh Gibson.

As she hands the ball to me she says, "There's nothing like baseball, baby, and I couldn't help but love it, especially that one time I got to hear the cheers, hear all the cheers, while stealing home."

Reader Response

Open for Discussion A little girl puts on her cousin Danny's shoes and plays baseball. Pretend you are there. Tell about that game.

1. Why do you suppose the author chose Josh Gibson as the baseball player Grandmama wants to be like?

2. Grandmama could not play baseball when she was young because she was a girl. How does that compare with girls' sports today?

3. Look back at page 309 and reread it. What picture did you have in your mind as you read this part? How did visualizing get you more involved in the story?

4. Work with a partner. Decide how you would explain the baseball terms *field*, *bases*, and *plate* to someone who doesn't know the game.

Look Back and Write Look back at pages 302 and 303. Josh Gibson hit a baseball in Pittsburgh. What happened to it? Use details from the story in your answer.

Angela Johnson

Read two more books by Angela Johnson.

Angela Johnson has written many great stories. Childhood memories of her father's baseball games inspired *Just Like Josh Gibson*. She says, "I remember the smell of the glove oil, the sound the bats made as the players tapped them on home plate, and the hot dogs I couldn't get enough of. Baseball is a wonderful memory for me. I wanted to write a book about it being a memory for another little girl."

Ms. Johnson recently won an important award to help her continue to write her wonderful stories.

Violet's Music

Do Like Kyla

Expository Nonfiction

Genre

- **Expository nonfiction explains an object or an idea.**

- **Expository nonfiction gives facts.**

Text Features

- **Headings, diagrams, captions, and charts or graphs are often used in nonfiction to help the reader better understand the text.**

- **This article includes picture graphs to show information about numbers of teams.**

Link to Social Studies
Use the library to find information about another game you want to learn about.

How Baseball Began

by Tammy Terry

illustrated by Clint Hansen

Baseball is called the national pastime of the United States. Hundreds of games are played and watched every spring and summer. But have you ever wondered how baseball began?

Who Invented It?

Well, no one knows for sure who invented the game. Many people believe that a man named Abner Doubleday invented baseball in 1839 in Cooperstown, New York.

Abner Doubleday

Baseball probably developed from the English game of the 1600s called "rounders."

Settlers living in America played rounders in the 1700s. They also called the game "town ball" and "base ball." Rules of the game varied from place to place. Over the years, the game of rounders became the game we now call baseball. One of the biggest differences between the two games is in how the batter is put out.

In rounders, players threw the ball at runners. If a runner got hit, he was out.

In baseball, players tag runners to put them out.

Compare and Contrast   What two games are being compared?

Players and Teams

The first official baseball game was played in Hoboken, New Jersey, on June 19, 1846. The New York Nine beat the Knickerbockers 23–1. More people became fans of the sport as more games were played.

In 1869, the Cincinnati Red Stockings became the first baseball team to get paid to play baseball. They won every game they played that year. Support for baseball continued to grow. More professional teams were formed. In 1876, eight teams joined to form the National League. The American League began in 1900 with eight teams.

YEAR	LEAGUE	TEAMS
1876	National	⚾ ⚾ ⚾ ⚾ ⚾ ⚾ ⚾ ⚾
1900	American	⚾ ⚾ ⚾ ⚾ ⚾ ⚾ ⚾ ⚾

Today, sixteen teams play in the National League. There are fourteen teams in the American League.

YEAR	LEAGUE	TEAMS
2005	National	⚾ ⚾ ⚾ ⚾ ⚾ ⚾ ⚾ ⚾ ⚾ ⚾ ⚾ ⚾ ⚾ ⚾ ⚾ ⚾
2005	American	⚾ ⚾ ⚾ ⚾ ⚾ ⚾ ⚾ ⚾ ⚾ ⚾ ⚾ ⚾ ⚾ ⚾

They play in cities across the United States **(1)** and Canada **(2)**. Each year, millions of people go to baseball games, watch the games on TV, and read about the teams in newspapers. The sport has spread throughout the world, and baseball is now played in countries such as Japan **(3)**, Italy **(4)**,and South Africa **(5)**.

Reading Across Texts

The story *Just Like Josh Gibson* tells that Grandmama played baseball in the 1940s. Use what you read in this article to figure out how long after the "invention" of baseball by Abner Doubleday that was.

Writing Across Texts Make a timeline to show the important dates in baseball history. Be sure to include the time when Grandmama played.

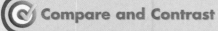 **Compare and Contrast** Use the charts to compare the number of teams in each league.

Using Capital Letters

Days of the week, months of the year, and **holidays** begin with capital letters.

Titles for people begin with capital letters.

Danny hurt his arm two days after the **Fourth of July**.

Mr. Gibson played baseball. I play baseball for **Coach** Johnson.

Write **Using Capital Letters**

1. Find a sentence in the story that uses more than one capital letter. Write the sentence. Underline the capital letters. Tell why the capital letters are there.

· ·

2. Three big holidays come during the baseball season: Memorial Day, the Fourth of July, and Labor Day. Which one of these holidays do you like best? Write a sentence about it. Use capital letters correctly.

· ·

3. What sport do you like? When is it played? Write a short paragraph about it. Use capital letters correctly.

321

Comprehension

Skill
Fact and Opinion

Strategy
Monitor
and Fix Up

Fact and Opinion

- A statement of fact can be proved true or false. You can look in a book, ask someone who knows, or see for yourself.

- A statement of opinion tells only someone's feelings or beliefs. It may have a clue word like *best* or *great.*

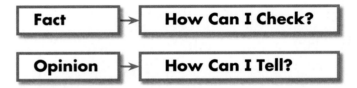

| Fact | → | How Can I Check? |
| Opinion | → | How Can I Tell? |

Strategy: Monitor and Fix Up

Active readers stop and fix up during reading. If you are not sure you are reading facts or opinions, you can go back and read again. See if a statement can be proved true or false. Look for a clue word to an opinion.

 **Write**

1. Read "Flags." Make charts like those above. Write down two facts and two opinions that you read.

2. Write two facts you know about the U.S. flag or another flag. Then write two of your opinions about it.

Flags

A flag is a piece of cloth. But it is also much more. A flag is a symbol. It can stand for a country. It is the best feeling to see your nation's flag flying.

A flag sends a message. Each picture and color on a flag tells something. A circle might mean the sun or life. Blue might stand for the sea or sky.

The first flags were metal or wooden poles. Later, pieces of cloth were added. Long ago, knights in armor carried flags. The flags helped them tell friends from enemies.

Today every country has a flag. Our country's flag is one of the most beautiful. Every state in our country has a flag too. Even some towns have flags.

Skill The clue word—*best*—signals an opinion. It tells only one person's feeling about seeing the flag flying.

Strategy If you are confused, go back and reread. If you're unsure, you can find out whether these facts are true. Where can you go to check?

323

Words to Know

nicknames

flag

stars

stripes

birthday

freedom

America

Remember

Try the strategy. Then, if you need more help, use your glossary or a dictionary.

Vocabulary Strategy
for Compound Words

Word Structure When you are reading, you may come to a long word. Do you see two small words in the long word? Then it is probably a compound word. You may be able to use the two small words to help you figure out the meaning of the compound word.

1. Divide the long word into its two small words.

2. Think of the meaning of each small word. Put the two meanings together. Does this help you understand the meaning of the compound word?

3. Try the meaning in the sentence. Does it make sense?

Read "America's Flag." Use the meanings of the small words to help you understand the meanings of the compound words.

AMERICA'S FLAG

★★★★★★★★★★★★★★★★★★★★★★★★★★★★★★★★

The Red, White, and Blue. The Stars and Stripes. These are nicknames for the American flag. You can probably guess why people call the flag by those names. Look at the picture of the flag. What colors do you see? You see red, white, and blue. What patterns do you see? You see stars and stripes.

People hang the flag outside their homes on special holidays like the Fourth of July. That is our country's birthday.

On that day long ago, the American colonies declared their freedom from England. But you don't have to wait for a holiday. You can fly your flag anytime you want. When you look at it, think about what it stands for—America and freedom.

Write about what the flag means to you. Use words from the Words to Know list.

Red, White, and Blue

★★★★★★ The Story of ★★★★★★
THE AMERICAN FLAG

★★★★★★★ BY ★★★★★★★

John Herman

ILLUSTRATED BY
Shannan Stirnweiss

Narrative nonfiction gives facts in the form of a story. Look for facts as you read.

How did the American flag change over the years?

We all know the American flag. Its bright colors fly at baseball games. It flies at Fourth of July parades. We even see it on clothes!

Our flag has lots of nicknames—like Old Glory and the Red, White, and Blue. Sometimes it's called the Stars and Stripes. But where did our flag come from? Who decided what it would look like? The truth is that no one knows for sure.

Back in the 1700s, America didn't have a flag. It didn't need one. It wasn't even a country yet.

It was just thirteen colonies. The colonies belonged to England. The English flag flew in towns from New Hampshire to Georgia.

But as time went on, the thirteen colonies didn't want to belong to England anymore. Americans decided to fight for their freedom.

A war began. It was the American Revolution. Now a new flag was needed—an American flag.

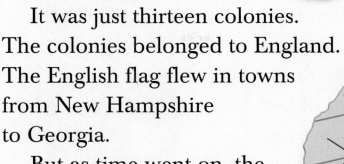

The original 13 American colonies

- New Hampshire
- Massachusetts
- Rhode Island
- Connecticut
- New York
- New Jersey
- Pennsylvania
- Delaware
- Maryland
- Virginia
- North Carolina
- South Carolina
- Georgia

Who made our first flag? Some people say it was a woman named Betsy Ross. Maybe you've heard of her. Betsy Ross owned a sewing shop in Philadelphia. She was famous for her sewing.

The story is that one day a general came to see her. The general was George Washington. He was the head of the American army.

General Washington wanted a new flag. It would make his soldiers feel like a real army fighting for a real country.

He wanted Betsy Ross to make this flag. He drew a picture of what he wanted.

Betsy Ross

George Washington

First American flag

Betsy Ross made some changes. Then she showed the picture to General Washington. He liked it!

Betsy Ross sewed the flag. And that was the very first Stars and Stripes.

That is the story—and it's a good one. But is it true? Betsy Ross's grandson said it was. He said that Betsy told him the story when he was a little boy and she was an old woman of eighty-four. But there is no proof for this story. So what do we know *for sure?*

We know that during the Revolution the colonists used lots of different flags.

Flags from the Revolutionary War

But once the colonies became the United States of America, the country needed *one* flag—the same flag for everybody.

So on June 14, 1777, a decision was made. The flag was going to have thirteen red and white stripes. The flag was also going to have thirteen white stars on a blue background, one for each of the thirteen colonies. Now the United States had a flag.

Congress had picked the colors and the stars and stripes. But Congress did not say where the stars and stripes had to go. So the flag still did not always look the same!

People could put them any way they liked. Sometimes the stripes were up and down, like this.

Sometimes the stars were in a circle, like this.

But nobody minded. Up and down or side to side, the stars and stripes still stood for the United States.

Over the years, the flag became more and more important to people.

In 1812, the United States was at war with England again. British soldiers came to America. They sailed up our rivers. They marched down our streets. They even burned down the White House—the home of the President.

Flag from battle at Fort McHenry

On the night of September 13, 1814, British soldiers bombed a fort in Maryland. All that night a man watched the fighting. His name was Francis Scott Key. He was afraid. What if the American soldiers in the fort gave up?

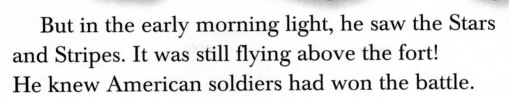

But in the early morning light, he saw the Stars and Stripes. It was still flying above the fort! He knew American soldiers had won the battle.

Key felt very proud. He wrote a poem about the flag on the fort. The poem was "The Star-Spangled Banner." Later the poem was put to music. This song about our flag became a song for our whole country.

Francis Scott Key

The flag that Francis Scott Key saw had fifteen stripes and fifteen stars.

Why? Because by then there were two more states—Vermont and Kentucky.

American flag in 1814

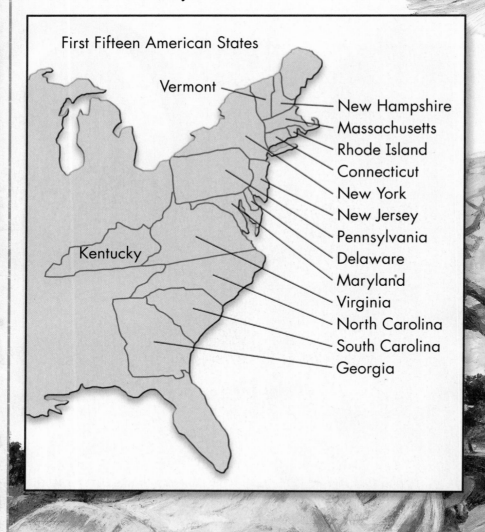

First Fifteen American States

Vermont

Kentucky

New Hampshire
Massachusetts
Rhode Island
Connecticut
New York
New Jersey
Pennsylvania
Delaware
Maryland
Virginia
North Carolina
South Carolina
Georgia

Our country was getting bigger. People were heading out west. In time, more places were going to want to be states. Soon there would be too many stripes to fit on the flag!

Congress had to do something. So in 1818 this is what was decided: The flag would go back to thirteen red and white stripes. And in the blue box would be one white star for each state. Every time there was a new state, a new star would be added.

At last the Stars and Stripes looked the same everywhere it flew. And Americans were proud of their flag. They took the flag with them as they moved west. The flag crossed the Mississippi River and the great grassy plains and the Rocky Mountains. It made it all the way to California.

More and more states were added to the country. And more and more stars were added to the flag. By 1837, there were twenty-six stars on the flag. By 1850, there were thirty-one.

Oregon Territory

Unorganized Territory

Utah Territory

CA

New Mexico Territory

American flag in 1850

The United States in 1850

This map shows all the states as of 1850.

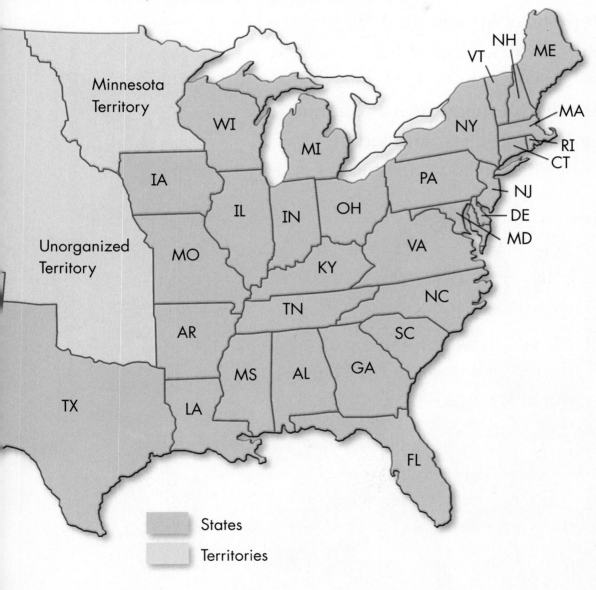

Minnesota Territory

Unorganized Territory

WI

MI

IA

IL

IN

OH

MO

KY

AR

TN

MS

AL

GA

LA

TX

FL

NH

VT

ME

NY

MA

RI

CT

PA

NJ

DE

MD

VA

NC

SC

States

Territories

One country. One flag. But then in 1861, something happened. Our country split in two. Eleven states in the South broke away from the United States of America. They started their own country. It was called the Confederate States of America.

Abraham Lincoln was President of the United States. He said *all* the states had to stay together.

President
Abraham Lincoln

War broke out—the Civil War. It was a very sad time in the history of our country.

The eleven southern states stopped flying the Stars and Stripes. They had their own flag.

In the North, some people wanted eleven stars taken off the Stars and Stripes. But Abraham Lincoln would not do that. He said the states would get back together. He was right. The Civil War ended in 1865. The North won. And the United States was one country under one flag again.

On June 14, 1877, the flag had a birthday—a big one. It was 100 years old. All across the country, people had picnics and parties and parades. June 14 became a holiday—Flag Day.

Today our flag has fifty stars for the fifty United States of America. Some flags are huge. One weighs 500 pounds! It is flown every Fourth of July from the George Washington Bridge.

342

The American flag flies in towns and cities from coast to coast.

And that's not all. In 1969, two American astronauts were the first people ever to land on the moon. The astronauts took lots of moon rocks back to Earth. They also left something on the moon . . . the Stars and Stripes.

And do you know what? Our flag is still flying there!

Reader Response

Open for Discussion What did you learn about the flag that you didn't know before? Talk about something that surprised you.

1. The author seems proud of the American flag. Read sentences that help show that he is proud.

2. Look for some facts and some opinions in the selection. Then write a fact and an opinion of your own about the flag.

3. Did anything in this selection confuse you? Where did you have a problem while reading? What did you do about it?

4. Create a bumper sticker to celebrate our country's flag. Use words from the Words to Know list and from the selection.

Look Back and Write Francis Scott Key wrote a poem. What is the name of the poem and why did he write it? Look back at pages 334 and 335. Use details from the selection in your answer.

Meet the Author

John Herman

Read more books about the American flag.

John Herman grew up near New York City. He knew he wanted to be a writer when he was 12 years old. Now he writes books for adults, teenagers, and children.

Mr. Herman likes to make up stories. *Red, White, and Blue* gave him a chance to write about real events. He loves reading about American history, so this was a new thing for him to try. He hopes to write more books like this in the future!

The Flag We Love by Pam Muñoz Ryan

Betsy Ross by Alexandra Wallner

Song

Genre

- **A song is a poem set to music.**

- **Songs often use rhyme. In each verse of this song, the first two lines rhyme, and the third and fifth lines rhyme.**

- **Songs often express the songwriter's feelings. As you read, think about how the songwriter feels about the flag.**

Link to Writing

Write words to a song about something you feel is important. It could be a poem set to a familiar tune. Share your song with your classmates.

You're a Grand Old Flag

by George M. Cohan

You're a grand old flag,

You're a high flying flag

And forever in peace may you wave.

You're the emblem of the land I love.

The home of the free and the brave.

Ev'ry heart beats true

'Neath the red, white, and blue,

Where there's never a boast or brag.

Should auld acquaintance be forgot,

Keep your eye on the grand old flag.

Reading Across Texts

"You're a Grand Old Flag" is one song about the flag of the United States. What other song about the flag did you read about in *Red, White, and Blue?*

Writing Across Texts Make a list of other patriotic songs that you know.

Monitor and Fix Up If you are confused, remember to go back and reread.

Quotation Marks

Quotation marks (" ") show the beginning and the end of the words someone says. The speaker's name and words such as **said** or **asked** are not inside the quotation marks.

"Can you make us a flag?" asked General Washington.

"I will try," Betsy Ross **said**.

Write Using Quotation Marks

1. Here is something Francis Scott Key might have said: Look. The flag is still there! Rewrite these sentences. Use quotation marks, the word *said,* and the name Francis Scott Key.

· ·

2. The picture on page 340 shows President Abraham Lincoln. He gave a speech about our country. What do you think he said? Write some sentences. Use quotation marks.

· ·

3. Pretend you are the astronaut who planted the flag on the moon. What would you say about your flag if a moon person walked by? Write some sentences. Use quotation marks.

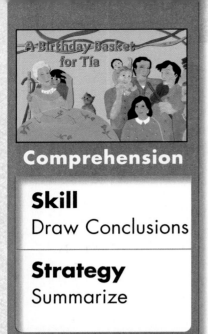

Comprehension

Skill
Draw Conclusions

Strategy
Summarize

Draw Conclusions

- When you read, you can draw conclusions or figure out more about the characters and what happens in a story.

- Use what you have read and what you know about real life.

- Find words in the text to support your ideas.

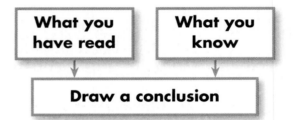

What you have read	What you know

Draw a conclusion

 ## Strategy: Summarize

Active readers summarize often to make sure they understand what they read. This will help you think about and draw conclusions.

1. Read "Empty Eggshells." Make a graphic organizer. Use it to draw conclusions about Jorge and Danny.

2. Write a short summary of the story. Tell who the main characters are and what they did.

Empty Eggshells

Jorge asked Danny to come early to his party. "Help me make cascarones," he said.

"What are cascarones?" Danny wondered.

When Danny arrived he saw a carton of eggs. But they were just eggshells with a hole at the top—no eggs inside.

"What do we do with these?" Danny asked.

"First, we will paint the eggshells. Next, we will fill each egg with tiny bits of paper," Jorge told him. "Then my mother will glue paper over each hole."

Before the party, Jorge's father hid the eggs in the apartment. All the children went on an egg hunt, and all the eggs were found. Then—surprise! Jorge cracked one open over the top of Danny's head! The colored paper rained down! Danny laughed and laughed. Soon everyone at the party was cracking cascarones on one another's heads!

Skill Here you can draw the conclusion that Jorge and Danny are best friends. Jorge asked Danny to come early and help.

Strategy You might want to stop here and sum up what you have read so far. Who are the characters and what did they do? Don't forget to sum up again at the end.

present

favorite

bank

basket

aunt

collects

Remember

Try the strategy. Then, if you need more help, use your glossary or a dictionary.

Vocabulary Strategy
for Homonyms

Context Clues When you read, you might come to a word you know, but the meaning doesn't make sense. The word may be a homonym. Homonyms are words that are pronounced and spelled the same but have different meanings. For example, *yard* means "space around a house." *Yard* also means "3 feet, or 36 inches." The words around the confusing word might help you.

1. If the meaning you know doesn't make sense, the word may be a homonym. Look at the nearby words.

2. Try to figure out another meaning for the homonym.

3. Try the meaning of the homonym in the sentence. Does it make sense?

Read "Picking a Present." Look for words that are homonyms. Use nearby words to figure out the meaning of each homonym.

Picking a Present

Is someone you know having a birthday soon? What will you give that person? It is not hard to think of a present. Ask yourself what the person likes. What is his or her favorite game? favorite hobby? favorite color? favorite food? See if the answers give you an idea.

You do not have to break your piggy bank to buy a present. Buy flowers at the grocery store. Find a basket or bowl at home. Arrange the flowers in it. This makes a nice present for your mother, grandmother, or aunt.

Make a picture frame out of cardboard or wood. Decorate it. Put a picture of you or your family in it. This makes a good present for your father, grandfather, or uncle. Maybe this special person collects things such as baseball cards, photos, or rings. Decorate a box that has a lid. Find or draw pictures that match what the person collects.

So start thinking now. That birthday will be here soon!

Write

Use your imagination. Write about a special gift you can give to a special friend or relative. Use words from the Words to Know list.

A Birthday Basket for Tía

by Pat Mora

illustrated by Cecily Lang

Genre **Realistic fiction** is a story with characters and events that are like people and events in real life.

What will be in the birthday basket for Tía?

Today is secret day. I curl my cat into my arms and say, "Ssshh, Chica. Can you keep our secret, silly cat?"

Today is special day. Today is my great-aunt's ninetieth birthday. Ten, twenty, thirty, forty, fifty, sixty, seventy, eighty, ninety. Ninety years old. *¡Noventa años!*

At breakfast Mamá asks, "What is today,
Cecilia?" I say, "Special day. Birthday day."

Mamá is cooking for the surprise party. I smell
beans bubbling on the stove. Mamá is cutting
fruit—pineapple, watermelon, mangoes. I sit in the
backyard and watch Chica chase butterflies. I hear
bees bzzzzz.

I draw pictures in the sand with a stick. I draw a
picture of my aunt, my *Tía*. I say, "Chica, what will
we give Tía?"

357

Chica and I walk around the front yard and the backyard looking for a good present. We walk around the house. We look in Mamá's room. We look in my closet and drawers.

I say, "Chica, shall we give her my little pots, my piggy bank, my tin fish, my dancing puppet?"

I say, "Mamá, can Chica and I use this basket?"

Mamá asks, "Why, Cecilia?"

"It's a surprise for the surprise party," I answer. Chica jumps into the basket. "No," I say. "Not for you, silly cat. This is a birthday basket for Tía."

I put a book in the basket. When Tía comes to our house, she reads it to me. It's our favorite book. I sit close to her on the sofa. I smell her perfume. Sometimes Chica tries to read with us. She sits on the book. I say, "Silly cat. Books are not for sitting."

I put Tía's favorite mixing bowl on the book in the basket. Tía and I like to make *bizcochos*, sugary cookies for the family.

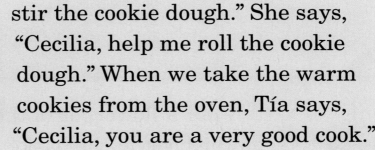

Tía says, "Cecilia, help me stir the cookie dough." She says, "Cecilia, help me roll the cookie dough." When we take the warm cookies from the oven, Tía says, "Cecilia, you are a very good cook."

I put a flowerpot in the mixing bowl on the book in the basket. Tía and I like to grow flowers for the kitchen window. Chica likes to put her face in the flowers. "Silly cat," I say.

I put a teacup in the flowerpot that is in the mixing bowl on the book in the basket. When I'm sick, my aunt makes me hot mint tea, *hierbabuena*. She brings it to me in bed. She brings me a cookie too.

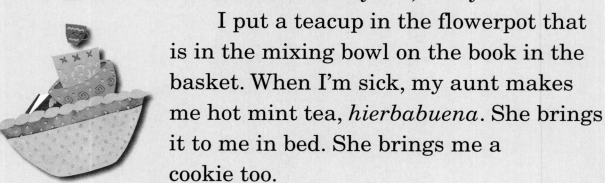

I put a red ball in the teacup that is in the flowerpot in the mixing bowl on the book in the basket. On warm days Tía sits outside and throws me the ball.

She says, "Cecilia, when I was a little girl in Mexico, my sisters and I played ball. We all wore long dresses and had long braids."

Chica and I go outside. I pick flowers to decorate Tía's basket. On summer days when I am swinging high up to the sky, Tía collects flowers for my room.

Mamá calls, "Cecilia, where are you?"

Chica and I run and hide our surprise.

I say, "Mamá, can you find the birthday basket for Tía?"

Mamá looks under the table. She looks in the refrigerator. She looks under my bed. She asks, "Chica, where is the birthday basket?"

Chica rubs against my closet door. Mamá and I laugh. I show her my surprise.

After my nap, Mamá and I fill a piñata with candy. We fill the living room with balloons. I hum, mmmmm, a little work song like the one Tía hums when she sets the table or makes my bed. I help Mamá set the table with flowers and tiny cakes.

"Here come the musicians," says Mamá. I open the front door. Our family and friends begin to arrive too.

I curl Chica into my arms. Then Mamá says, "Sshh, here comes Tía."

I rush to open the front door. "Tía! Tía!" I shout. She hugs me and says,

"Cecilia, *¿qué pasa?* What is this?"

"SURPRISE!" we all shout. "¡*Feliz cumpleaños!* Happy birthday!" The musicians begin to play their guitars and violins.

"Tía! Tía!" I say, "It's special day, birthday day!
It's your ninetieth birthday surprise party!"
Tía and I laugh.

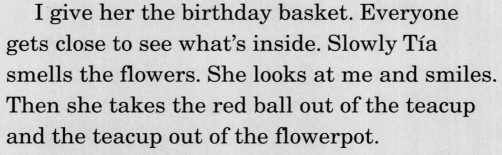

I give her the birthday basket. Everyone gets close to see what's inside. Slowly Tía smells the flowers. She looks at me and smiles. Then she takes the red ball out of the teacup and the teacup out of the flowerpot.

She pretends to take a sip of tea and we all laugh.

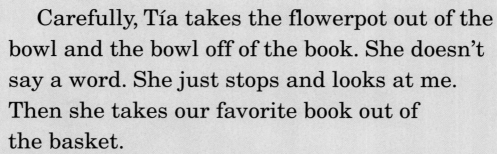

Carefully, Tía takes the flowerpot out of the bowl and the bowl off of the book. She doesn't say a word. She just stops and looks at me. Then she takes our favorite book out of the basket.

And guess who jumps into the basket?

Chica. Everyone laughs.

Then the music starts and my aunt surprises me. She takes my hands in hers. Without her cane, she starts to dance with me.

Reader Response

Open for Discussion Pretend you made a birthday basket for someone. What six things would you put into it? Why?

1. Authors like to put surprises into stories. What are the surprises in *A Birthday Basket for Tía*? Were you surprised, or did you guess?

2. Think about the things Cecilia put into the basket for Tía. What conclusions can you draw about how Cecilia feels about her Tía?

3. Look back at page 362. Summarize what has happened so far in the story.

4. Presents go with birthday parties. What other words in the story could go on a list of "party" words?

Look Back and Write What did Cecilia *first* think she might give to Tía? What things did Cecilia finally give to Tía? Make two lists. Use details from the story in your answer.

Pat Mora

Read two more books by Pat Mora.

This Big Sky

Though Pat Mora grew up in Texas, she came from a home where both English and Spanish were spoken. When she started writing books, Ms. Mora realized she wanted to write about her experience as a Mexican American. "It was like opening a treasure chest," Ms. Mora says. "My whole Mexican heritage was something I could write about."

Ms. Mora tells students to write about what they love. She says, "The trick is how we bring everything that we are to the page—everything."

Tomás and the Library Lady

Reading Online

Online Directories

Genre

- Online directories give links to Web sites about a topic you choose.

- You can use an online directory or a search engine to learn about a topic.

Text Features

- Directories list links to many topics. You may click on any link.

- Or you may type in a keyword and then click on the search button.

- Then you will get a list of links to Web sites about your topic.

Link to Social Studies

- Interview members of your family about family traditions they remember celebrating.

Take It to the NET
ONLINE

more activities sfsuccessnet.com

Family Traditions: Birthdays

How can you find out more about birthdays? You can go to an Internet online directory. Here are some of the topics you might find listed there.

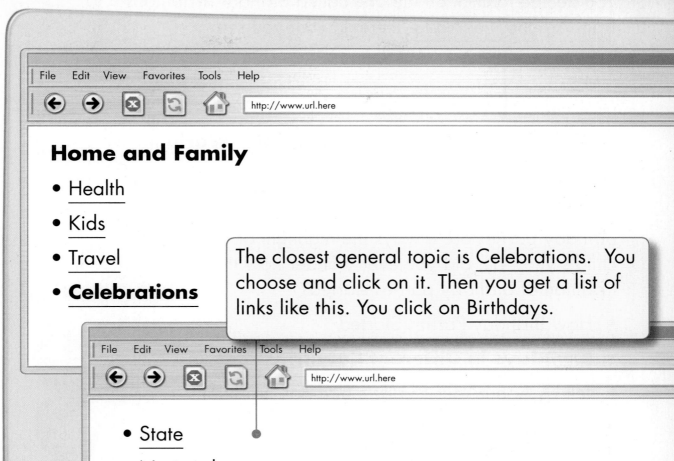

Home and Family

- Health
- Kids
- Travel
- **Celebrations**

The closest general topic is Celebrations. You choose and click on it. Then you get a list of links like this. You click on Birthdays.

- State
- National
- Fairs
- **Birthdays**

Summarize   Sum up what you've read so far.

When you click on Birthdays, you get a list of Web sites. You decide to click on the one called Birthday Traditions from Around the World. Here is what you see:

File   Edit   View   Favorites   Tools   Help

http://www.url.here

Birthday Traditions from Around the World

Discover how the tradition of birthdays started. Find out how people in other countries celebrate birthdays.

Birthday parties are always the highlight of a child's year, but did you ever wonder how the tradition of birthday parties started?

- How Birthday Parties Started
- **Birthdays in Different Countries**
- Tell Us About Your Family's Birthday Traditions
- See a Listing of Birthday Party Places
- Find a Birthday Present
- Find Out What Famous People Share Your Birth Date
- Children's Book and Video Store
- Birthday Related Products and Links
- Go to the Kids Parties Connection Home Page

You click on the link Birthdays in Different Countries. You can read about some of these traditions on the next page.

Birthdays in Different Countries

Canada—In some parts of Canada, birthday children get their noses greased for good luck. Greased noses make children too slippery for bad luck to catch them.

China—People are invited to lunch. Noodles are served to wish the birthday child a long life.

Cuba—The parties are similar to those in the United States. Food, decorations, gifts, piñatas, cake, candles, the Happy Birthday song, and games are included.

India—At school, the birthday child wears a colored dress and passes out chocolates to the entire class.

Vietnam—Everyone's birthday is celebrated on New Year's Day, called Tet. The Vietnamese do not celebrate the exact day they were born. A baby turns one on Tet no matter when he or she was born that year.

Reading Across Texts

Compare the birthday celebration in *A Birthday Basket for Tía* to the ones listed above. Which is most like Tía's celebration? Which are most different?

Writing Across Texts Make a chart to show your comparisons.

 **Draw Conclusions** What conclusions can you draw about birthdays?

Using Commas

Commas are used in addresses.
123 Hermana Road
San Antonio, TX 55555

Commas are used in dates.
May 23, 1939
Monday, June 20

Commas are used to begin and end
a letter.
Dear Cecilia,
Yours truly,

Commas are used to separate three or
more things in a sentence.
Cecilia gave Tía a flower, a book,
and a mixing bowl.

Write Using Commas

1. Find a sentence in *A Birthday Basket for Tía* that uses commas to separate three or more things. Write the sentence. Circle the commas.

- -

2. Cecilia gathered many things for Tía's birthday basket. Write a sentence listing three things you would give to someone as a birthday surprise. Use commas in your sentence.

- -

3. You are Tía. Write a thank you letter to Cecilia for your birthday basket. Be sure your letter has a date. Use commas correctly.

COWBOYS

Comprehension

Skill
Cause and Effect

Strategy
Graphic
Organizers

Cause and Effect

- As you read, look for what happened and why it happened.
- Clue words help you figure out what happened and why. *Because*, *so*, and *since* are clue words.

Strategy: Graphic Organizers

Good readers use graphic organizers. A graphic organizer can help you understand what you read. A chart like this one can help you keep track of what happened and why it happened.

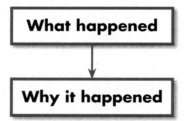

Write

1. Read "The Stagecoach Driver." Look for clue words that tell what happened and why it happened.

2. Make a chart like the one above. Fill in your chart to show what happened and why it happened.

THE STAGECOACH DRIVER

Being a stagecoach driver was a hard job. A driver had to take care of a stagecoach full of people. A stagecoach would sometimes get stuck or tip over because it traveled on muddy trails and rocky roads. And sometimes stagecoaches were robbed.

Charley Parkhurst was a stagecoach driver. He was a small person with a patch over one eye. He did not talk much. Charley drove stagecoaches for 20 years. When he died, people found out that Charley was a woman!

Charlotte Parkhurst wanted to drive a stagecoach. But women were not allowed, so Charlotte changed her name to Charley. She put on men's clothes. For 20 years she acted like a man. No one knew her secret.

Skill Here is a clue word —*because*. It signals a cause and effect. It tells why stagecoaches sometimes got stuck or tipped over.

Strategy Here is another clue word—*so*. If you made a graphic organizer, what would you write in it?

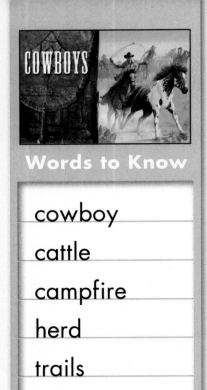

COWBOYS

Words to Know

cowboy

cattle

campfire

herd

trails

railroad

galloped

Remember

Try the strategy. Then, if you need more help, use your glossary or a dictionary.

Vocabulary Strategy
for Compound Words

Word Structure When you are reading, you may come across a long word that you don't know. If the long word is made up of two small words, then it is probably a compound word. The two small words can help you figure out the meaning of the compound word.

1. Look for the two small words in a long word.

2. Think about what each small word means. Put those meanings together. Does this help you understand the compound word?

3. Try the new meaning in the sentence. Does it make sense?

Read "Like a Cowboy." Look for compound words. Use the meanings of the small words in each compound word to help you figure out the new meaning.

378

LIKE A COWBOY

What was it like to be a cowboy long ago? To find out, some people stay on a ranch. They ride horses, and they chase and rope cattle, or cows. At night around a campfire, they tell stories and sing songs. They even take a herd of cattle on a cattle drive.

Long ago, cowboys took herds of cattle on cattle drives. They traveled on trails that ran from Texas to Kansas. From there, railroad trails took the cattle to cities in the East. The trail was a thousand miles long. The cattle drive lasted for months.

The cattle drive at the ranch today lasts only a day or two. Still, the cattle drive gives people an idea of what it was like to be a cowboy. They can imagine how hard the cowboys worked on the trail. They can imagine how happy the cowboys were as they galloped into town after a long cattle drive.

Write

Would you like to be a cowboy or a cowgirl? Why or why not? Write your ideas. Use words from the Words to Know list.

COWBOYS

by Lucille Recht Penner
illustrated by Ben Carter

Genre **Narrative Nonfiction** gives information about the real world. Look for facts about cowboys.

What was it like to live as a cowboy?

If you were out west about a hundred years ago, you might have heard a cowboy yelling—*ti yi yippy yay!*—as he rode across the plains.

What was it like to be a cowboy way back then?

Cowboys lived on cattle ranches. A ranch had a house for the rancher and his family, barns for animals, and a bunkhouse where the cowboys slept.

The rancher owned thousands of cattle. They wandered for miles looking for grass and water.

Twice a year, the cowboys drove all the cattle together. This was called a roundup. The cowboys counted the baby calves that had been born since the last roundup. The biggest cattle were chosen to sell at market.

A roundup was hard work. The cattle were wild and fast. They had long, sharp, dangerous horns. Cowboys called them Longhorns. If you made a Longhorn mad, it would charge at you. A cowboy didn't want to get close to an angry Longhorn.

So he made a loop in the end of his rope. Then he twirled it over his head and let it fly. When he caught the Longhorn, he could tell that it belonged to his ranch.

How could he tell? It was easy. Each rancher put a special mark called a brand on his cows. Baby calves didn't have brands, yet. They didn't need them. A baby calf always followed its mother.

Every ranch had its own name and its own brand. The Rocking Chair Ranch brand looked like a rocking chair. The Flying V Ranch brand looked like this:

After the roundup was over, it was time to sell the Longhorns. That meant taking them to big market towns. Back then, there were no roads across the wide plains—only dusty trails that cattle had made with their hooves as they tramped along. Some trails were a thousand miles long! Since cattle could walk only fifteen miles a day, the long, hard trip often lasted months. It was called a trail drive. There was a lot to do to get ready.

At the beginning of a trail day, one cowboy rode out in front of the herd. "Come on, boys," he called

to the cattle. A few big Longhorns started after him. They bellowed and swung their heads from side to side. Other cattle followed, and soon they were all on their way.

Cattle didn't like so much walking. After a while, they wanted to turn around and go home. Cowboys rode up and down the sides of the herd to keep them in line. A few cowboys rode at the end of the herd to make sure no cattle were left behind.

It was hot on the trail. Cowboys wore hats
with wide brims to keep the sun out of their eyes.
When it rained, the brims made good umbrellas.
Around their necks, cowboys wore red bandannas.
When it got dusty, they pulled the bandannas
over their noses.

Leather leggings—called chaps—were tied over
their pants to keep out thorns and cactus spines.

High leather boots kept out dirt and pebbles.
Cowboy boots had handles called "mule ears."
The cowboy grabbed the mule ears to pull his
boots off and on.

What else did a cowboy need on his trail? A good horse. Cowboys spent the whole day on horseback. They rode little horses called cow ponies. A good cow pony was fearless. It could cross rough ground in the blackest night. It could swim a deep, wide river.

It could crash right through the bushes after a runaway cow. The cowboy had to hold on tight!

Every day the herd tramped the hot, dry plains. Two or three big steers were the leaders. They always walked in front. The cowboys got to know them well. They gave them pet names, like "Old Grumpy" and "Starface."

Cows could get in trouble. Sometimes one got stuck in the mud. The cowboy roped it and pulled it out. A cow might get hurt on the trail. A cowboy took care of that, too.

At night the cowboys stopped to let the cattle eat, drink, and sleep. It was time for the cowboys to eat, too. "Cookie" had a hot meal ready for them. That's what cowboys called the cook.

Cookie drove a special wagon called the chuckwagon. It had drawers for flour, salt, beans, and pots and pans. A water barrel was tied underneath.

Cookie gave every cowboy a big helping of biscuits, steak, gravy, and beans. He cooked the

same meal almost every night, but the cowboys didn't mind. It tasted good!

There were no tables or chairs, so the cowboys sat right on the ground. After dinner they played cards or read by the flickering light of the campfire. The nights were chilly and bright with stars.

But the cowboys didn't stay up late. They were tired. At bedtime, they just pulled off their boots and crawled into their bedrolls. A cowboy never wore pajamas. What about a pillow? He used his saddle.

Trail drives were dangerous. Many things could go wrong. The herd might stampede if there was a loud noise—like a sudden crash of thunder. A stampede was scary. Cattle ran wildly in all directions, rolling their eyes and bellowing with fear. The ground shook under them. The bravest cowboys galloped to the front of the herd. They had to make

the leaders turn. They shouted at them and fired
their six shooters in the air. They tried to make the
cattle run in a circle until they calmed down.

Sometimes they'd run into rustlers. A rustler was
a cow thief. Rustlers hid behind rocks and jumped
out at the cattle to make them stampede. While the
cowboys were trying to catch the terrified cattle and
calm them down, the rustlers drove off as many as
they could.

When the herd came to a big river, the cowboys in front galloped right into the water. The cattle plunged in after them. The cattle swam mostly under water. Sometimes the cowboys could see only the tips of their black noses and their long white horns.

Most cowboys didn't know how to swim. If a cowboy fell into the water, he grabbed the horse's tail and held on tight until they reached shore.

Trail drives often went through Indian Territory. The Indians charged ten cents a head to let the cattle cross their land. If the cowboys didn't pay, there might be a fight. But usually the money was handed over and the herd plodded on.

At last, the noisy, dusty cattle stamped into a market town. The cowboys drove them into pens near the railroad tracks. Then they got their pay. It was time for fun!

What do you think most cowboys wanted first? A bath! The barber had a big tub in the back of the shop. For a dollar, you could soak and soak. A boy kept throwing in pails of hot water. Ahh-h-h! Next it was time for a shave, a haircut, and some new clothes.

Tonight, the cowboys would sleep in real beds and eat dinner at a real table. They would sing, dance, and have fun with their friends.

But soon they would be heading back to Longhorn country. There would be many more hot days in the saddle. There would be many more cold nights under the stars.

SOME CATTLE TRAILS OF THE OLD WEST

KEY

— Western Trail

— Chisholm Trail

— Sedalia Trail

Nebraska
● Ogallala

Kansas
Ellsworth   ● Abilene

Missouri
● Sedalia

Dodge City ●

Arkansas

Oklahoma

● Dallas

Texas

Louisiana

Brownsville ●

● Houston

San Antonio ●

N
W ◆ E
S

Reader Response

Open for Discussion Would you have liked a cowboy's job? What part would have been fun? What part might have made you pack up your gear and go away?

1. Suppose you could ask the author why she decided to write about cowboys. Think of three good reasons she might tell you.

2. What effect might a noisy thunderstorm have during a trail drive? Look back on pages 394 and 395 to help you answer.

3. If you made a graphic organizer as you read, how did it help you? If you didn't, what would you suggest to someone who is about to read it?

4. Here are some compound words from the story: *bunkhouse, bedrolls, longhorns, horseback, runaway, haircut.* Use one of the two small words in each to make a new compound word.

Look Back and Write A list of "Trail Drive Dangers" might have helped cowboys. Make a list for them. Use information on pages 391 to 397 to help you.

Read other books written by Lucille Recht Penner or illustrated by Ben Carter.

Lucille Recht Penner often writes about life long ago. She tries to show how "people just like you" lived in the past. Ms. Penner likes to write about cowboys. People were adventurous and brave in the Old West. They were willing to do hard things even when they didn't know what would happen to them.

Ms. Penner reads many books about a subject before she begins writing. Then she chooses the most interesting and unusual parts to include in the book.

Ben Carter has been an artist since he graduated from college. He is of Native American descent, and his books often draw upon his heritage.

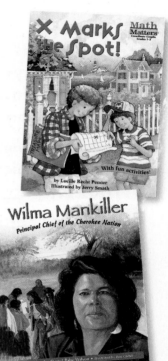

X Marks the Spot!

Wilma Mankiller: Principal Chief of the Cherokee Nation

Picture Encyclopedia

Genre

- Picture encyclopedias provide information on many topics.
- There are many photos or pictures with captions.
- A reader can read the captions in any order.

Text Features

- In this article, the picture shows what a cowboy wears.
- The captions explain more about each part of a cowboy's outfit.

Link to Social Studies

Use the library or the Internet to find out more about cowboy equipment. Share your findings with the class.

COWBOY GEAR

from *The Cowboy's Handbook*

★ by Tod Cody ★

A cowboy's clothes and equipment had to be hard-wearing. There was no room for luggage on the trail drive, and most cowboys wore the same thing for months. Mud-caked and smelly, these clothes were often burned at the end of the journey.

READY TO HIT THE TRAIL!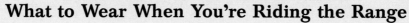
What to Wear When You're Riding the Range

HAT

You can use it to signal to other cowboys, beat trail dust off your clothes, and hold food for your horse. A true cowboy wears his hat when he's sleeping.

PANTS

Cowboys originally refused to wear jeans because they were worn by miners and farm laborers. Pants (trousers) made of thick woolen material are more comfortable to wear on horseback.

BOOTS

The pointed toes and high heels are designed for riding, not for walking. That's why cowboys in the movies walk the way they do!

BANDANNA

Soak it in water, roll it up into a wad, and place it under your hat to keep cool during a hot spell. You can also use it to filter muddy water and blindfold a "spooked" horse.

CHAPS

These thick leather leg-coverings will protect your legs from cow horns, rope burns, scrapes, and scratches. They also give a better grip to the saddle.

Reading Across Texts

What different information did each selection give about hats, bandannas, chaps, and boots?

Writing Across Texts

Write a paragraph explaining which piece of gear you think cowboys needed most.

 Cause and Effect   What effect do boots have on a cowboy's walk?

Commas in Compound Sentences

Sometimes two sentences have ideas that go together. These sentences can be combined using a comma and a connecting word, such as **and** or **but**. The combined sentence is called a **compound sentence**.

A cowpony crossed rough ground. It swam deep rivers.

A cowpony crossed rough ground**, and** it swam deep rivers.

Cows get stuck in mud. Cowboys pull them out.

Cows get stuck in mud**, but** cowboys pull them out.

Write **Using Commas in Compound Sentences**

1. Use a comma and the word *and* to combine these two sentences.

A cow might get hurt on the trail.

A cowboy takes care of that too.

· ·

2. Cowboys did many things. Think about things you like to do. Write a compound sentence using a comma and the word *but* or *and*.

· ·

3. What are some facts you learned about cowboys? Write a short paragraph telling some things you learned. Include at least one compound sentence.

Character, Setting, Plot

A story has characters, a plot, and a setting.

- Characters can be animals or people. An author tells about the characters.
- The setting tells where and when a story takes place.
- The plot is what happens throughout the story.

Story Title		
Characters	**Setting**	**Plot**
		beginning:
		middle:
		end:

Strategy: Prior Knowledge

Good readers use what they already know to help them understand what they read. As you read, use what you know to help you understand the characters and the plot.

1. Read "Powwow!" Make a chart like the one above to describe each part of the story.

2. Choose one thing about "Powwow!" that reminds you of something or someone you know. Write about it.

POWWOW!

Mike's family could not often spend much time together. Mike had drum lessons. His sister played soccer. His mother and father had jobs. They were all very busy.

"Come on," his father called one day. "We are all going to the powwow." Once a year, Mike's family and other Native Americans came together for this big fair.

At the powwow they watched the Fancy Shawl dancing. Then they walked all around. They saw the beautiful art and jewelry. They stopped at Aunt Numa's stand to get fry bread with beans and cheese. "Are you up for a big night of dancing and singing?" she asked.

"Yes!" was their answer.

It was dark when the family left. Tomorrow Mike would have his drum lesson. His sister had a soccer game. His mother and father would go to work. But today, at the powwow, they had fun being together.

Strategy Does this remind you of anything you are familiar with? Use what you know to help you understand this family.

Skill This is a good spot to ask yourself: Who are the characters in the story? Where does the story take place?

drum

clattering

voice

jingles

silver

borrow

Remember

Try the strategy. Then, if you need more help, use your glossary or a dictionary.

Vocabulary Strategy
for Unfamiliar Words

Context Clues When you come to a word you don't know during reading, what can you do? You can look for clues in the words and sentences around the word. This strategy can help you figure out the meaning of the word.

1. Read the words and sentences around the word you don't know. Sometimes the author gives you an explanation.

2. If not, predict a meaning for the word.

3. Try that meaning in the sentence. Does it make sense?

Read "Fiona's Feet." Look for clues in nearby words and sentences to help you understand the meanings of the vocabulary words.

Fiona's Feet

Fiona loves to dance. As soon as she hears the sounds of the fiddle, the pipes, and the drum, her feet start to move. When Fiona wears her hard shoes, her feet make a clattering noise. Tap, tap, tappity, tappity, tap. It is as though her feet are talking in a loud, happy voice. But when Fiona wears her soft shoes, her feet make no noise at all. That is the way it is supposed to be. But Fiona wishes her feet had a voice then too.

One morning as Fiona was eating her porridge, her sister walked into the kitchen. Fiona heard a faint sound, like the jingles of a bell. The sound made her think of snowflakes.

"Moira," asked Fiona, "what is making that sound?"

Moira showed Fiona her earrings. They were tiny silver bells that jingled when Moira walked. Fiona had an idea.

"May I borrow the bells?" she asked.

That night when Fiona danced in her soft shoes, her feet made a tinkling sound. Jingle, jingle, jingle, jingle. It was as though her feet were talking in a small, sweet voice.

Write

Describe something else that jingles. Use words from the Words to Know list.

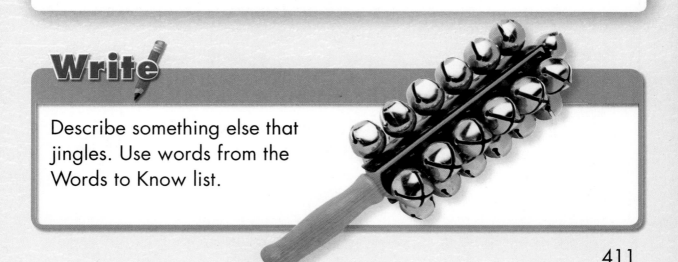

Jingle Dancer

by Cynthia Leitich Smith
illustrated by Cornelius Van Wright and Ying-Hwa Hu

Will Jenna get enough jingles for her outfit?

Tink, tink, tink, tink, sang cone-shaped jingles sewn to Grandma Wolfe's dress. Every Grandma bounce-step brought clattering *tinks* as light blurred silver against jingles of tin.

Jenna daydreamed at the kitchen table, tasting honey on fry bread, her heart beating to the *brum, brum, brum, brum* of the powwow drum.

As Moon kissed Sun good night, Jenna shifted her head on Grandma Wolfe's shoulder. "I want to jingle dance, too."

"Next powwow, you could dance Girls," Grandma Wolfe answered. "But we don't have enough time to mail-order tins for rolling jingles."

Again and again, Jenna watched a videotape of Grandma Wolfe jingle dancing. When Grandma bounce-stepped on TV, Jenna bounce-stepped on family room carpet.

But Jenna's dress would not be able to sing. It needed four rows of jingles.

As Sun fetched morning, Jenna danced east to Great-aunt Sis's porch. Jenna's bounce-steps crunched autumn leaves, but her steps didn't jingle.

Once again, Great-aunt Sis told Jenna a Muscogee Creek story about Bat. Although other animals had said he was too small to make a difference, Bat won a ball game by flying high and catching a ball in his teeth.

Rising sunlight reached through a windowpane and flashed against . . . what was it, hanging in Aunt Sis's bedroom?

Jingles on a dress too long quiet.

"May I borrow enough jingles to make a row?" Jenna asked, not wanting to take so many that Aunt Sis's dress would lose its voice.

"You may," Aunt Sis answered, rubbing her calves. "My legs don't work so good anymore. Will you dance for me?"

"I will," said Jenna with a kiss on Aunt Sis's cheek.

Now Jenna's dress needed three more rows.

As Sun arrived at midcircle, Jenna skipped south to Mrs. Scott's brand-new duplex. At Jenna's side, jingles clinked.

Mrs. Scott led Jenna into the kitchen. Once again, Jenna rolled dough, and Mrs. Scott fried it.

"May I borrow enough jingles to make a row?" Jenna asked, not wanting to take so many that Mrs. Scott's dress would lose its voice.

"You may," Mrs. Scott answered, tossing flour with her apron. "At powwow, I'll be busy selling fry bread and Indian tacos. Will you dance for me?"

"I will," said Jenna with a high five.

Now Jenna's dress needed two more rows.

As Sun caught a glimpse of Moon, Jenna strolled west to Cousin Elizabeth's apartment. At Jenna's side, jingles clanked.

Elizabeth had arrived home late from the law firm. Once again, Jenna helped Elizabeth carry in her files.

"May I borrow enough jingles to make a row?" Jenna asked, not wanting to take so many that Elizabeth's dress would lose its voice.

"You may," Elizabeth answered, burrowing through her messy closet for her jingle dress. "This weekend, I'm working on a big case and can't go to powwow. Will you dance for me?"

"I will," said Jenna, clasping her cousin's hands.

Now Jenna's dress needed one more row of jingles, but she didn't know which way to turn.

As Moon glowed pale, Jenna shuffled north to Grandma Wolfe's. At Jenna's side, jingles sat silent. High above, clouds wavered like worried ghosts.

When Jenna tugged open the door, jingles sang, *tink, tink, tink, tink.* Grandma Wolfe was jingle dancing on TV. Jenna breathed in every *hey-ah-ho-o* of a powwow song. Her heart beat *brum, brum, brum, brum* to the pounding of the drum.

On family room carpet, beaded moccasins waited for Jenna's feet. She shucked off a sneaker and slipped on a moccasin that long before had danced with Grandma Wolfe.

Jenna knew where to find her fourth row.

"May I borrow enough jingles to make a row?" Jenna asked, not wanting to take so many that Grandma Wolfe's dress would lose its voice.

"You may," Grandma said with a hug.

Now Jenna's dress could sing.

Every night that week, Jenna helped Grandma Wolfe sew on jingles and bring together the dance regalia.

Every night, Jenna practiced her bounce-steps.

Brum, brum, brum, brum, sounded the drum at the powwow the next weekend. As light blurred silver, Jenna jingle danced

. . . for Great-aunt Sis, whose legs ached,

. . . for Mrs. Scott, who sold fry bread,

. . . for Elizabeth, who
worked on her big case,

. . . and for Grandma Wolfe,
who warmed like Sun.
Tink, tink, tink, tink.

Reader Response

Open for Discussion *Tink, tink, brum, brum.* These are important sounds in the story. Use the sounds as you tell about Jenna, the jingle dancer.

1. The author lets you know that the story happens now instead of long ago. How does she let you know that?

2. Who is Jenna, where is she, and what problem does she have? How did she solve her problem?

3. What did you already know about Native Americans that helped you understand the story?

4. Draw a row of jingles like those in the story. On each jingle, write a "sound" word from the story. One example might be *tink*. Remember to include words from the Words to Know list.

Test Practice

Look Back and Write Why didn't Jenna get all four rows of jingles from one person's dress? Look back at the story. Use details from the story in your answer.

Read more books by Cynthia Leitich Smith or illustrated by Mr. Van Wright and Ms. Hu.

Cynthia Leitich Smith is a member of the Creek Nation, just like Jenna in *Jingle Dancer.* "*Jingle Dancer* was one of my first stories for young readers. I had gone to law school. But at my first job, I found myself scribbling stories during my lunch hour. My real dream was to become a fiction writer. So I did."

Indian Shoes

Mei-Mei Loves the Morning

Cornelius Van Wright and **Ying-Hwa Hu** are a husband-and-wife artist team. Mr. Van Wright says about children's art, "There are so many different kinds of kids—all kinds of shapes and sizes. What beauty! What freedom!"

427

Photo Essay

Genre

- **A photo essay includes text and many photos on one topic.**

Text Features

- **In this selection, the photos show what happens during Buffalo Days.**

- **The captions tell about the photos.**

Link to Social Studies

Use the library or the Internet to find out about other powwow activities. Organize a classroom powwow to talk about the rules and affairs of your classroom.

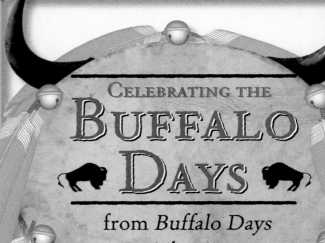

CELEBRATING THE

BUFFALO DAYS

from *Buffalo Days*

✿ by ✿

Diane Hoyt-Goldsmith

Every summer the Crow nation holds a special gathering to celebrate the Buffalo Days. The Crow Fair and Rodeo is something that everyone looks forward to all year long. The fair began in 1904 as a way to encourage ranching and farming. Over the years, it has become a celebration of Native American traditions. People who come to the fair are able to experience a way of life that existed during the Buffalo Days.

The Crow Fair and Rodeo is called the Tipi Capital of the World. People put up more than a thousand tipis on the fairgrounds.

During the third week in August, Crow people from all over the reservation gather to put up their tipis. They hold a powwow that lasts for many days, with dance contests, drumming, and giveaways. There are rodeo competitions and horse races every day. People from other tribes all over North America come to share in the fun.

Graphic Organizers If it will help, make a graphic organizer.

Each day during the Crow Fair, hundreds of Native American dancers from all over the West compete in different categories. People of all ages come to perform and to watch. For everyone, it is a time to celebrate the best of their traditions and to keep those traditions alive.

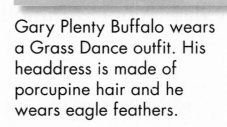

Gary Plenty Buffalo wears a Grass Dance outfit. His headdress is made of porcupine hair and he wears eagle feathers.

Kalsey BirdinGround wears a Jingle Dance dress. The jingles on her dress are made from the tops of tin cans that have been shaped into cones.

Marilyn Blacksmith wears an outfit for the Fancy Shawl Dance. There are mink tails braided into her hair, and she wears a white eagle feather.

Marcia Blacksmith wears a traditional Crow dress decorated with elk teeth. She holds a fan of hawk feathers and a handbag decorated with beadwork.

Reading Across Texts

Modern Native American powwows celebrate old traditions. What are some that you read about in *Jingle Dancer* and in this selection?

Writing Across Texts

Make a list of traditions celebrated at powwows. If you wish, draw pictures to illustrate your list.

Graphic Organizers What can you add to your graphic organizer?

The Paragraph

A **paragraph** is a group of sentences about the same idea. The sentences are in an order that makes sense. One sentence gives the main idea. The other sentences give details about the main idea. The first sentence of a paragraph is indented.

Jenna's dress needed four rows of jingles. One row came from Aunt Sis. Another came from Mrs. Scott. A third row came from Elizabeth. The last row of jingles came from Grandma Wolfe. Now Jenna could dance at the powwow.

Write  Using Paragraphs

1. Write the sentence that doesn't belong in this paragraph. Tell why it doesn't belong.

   Jenna wanted to jingle dance. She knew she could do it. She watched the videotape of Grandma Wolfe over and over. She ate fry bread at the table. She bounce-stepped on the carpet, just like Grandma Wolfe.

· ·

2. Think about a performance you have seen. Write a paragraph to tell about it. Underline the main idea. Indent the first sentence.

· ·

3. Find some facts about powwows. Write a short report about what you find out. Include a main idea sentence and detail sentences. Indent your paragraphs.

Wrap-Up

A Grand New Flag

connect to

ART

Design a flag for your family. Think about what colors might help show something important. What symbols or pictures would help others learn about your family? Paint your design. Then show your flag to a friend. Explain what you want it to show.

How are traditions and celebrations important to our lives?

A Curious Culture

connect to WRITING

You read about many cultures and traditions in this unit. Which one did you find most interesting or surprising? Write a paragraph or two about it. Tell what you learned that was important.

Cowboys

Another Birthday Basket

connect to SOCIAL STUDIES

Suppose a character you read about in *Just Like Josh Gibson* or in *Jingle Dancer* wanted to make a present as the girl did in *A Birthday Basket for Tía*. Who would the character make it for? What would the present be? Why would the person like it? Draw a picture of the present. Tell a partner about it.

Glossary

Aa

America

adventure (uhd VEN cher) An **adventure** is an exciting or unusual thing to do: Riding a raft down the river was a great **adventure**. *NOUN*

afternoon (af ter NOON) The **afternoon** is the part of the day between morning and evening: On Saturday we played all **afternoon**. *NOUN*

America (uh MAIR uh kuh) **America** is another name for North **America**. Some people use the name **America** to mean the United States. *NOUN*

American Revolution (uh MAIR uh kuhn rev uh LOO shuhn) The **American Revolution** was a series of protests and acts of American colonists from 1763 to 1783 against England. It is also known as the Revolutionary War.

angry (ANG gree) If you are **angry**, you feel upset or mad: Dad was **angry** when he saw the broken car window. *ADJECTIVE*

assistant (uh SIS tuhnt) An **assistant** is a helper: I was her **assistant** in the library. *NOUN*

aunt (ANT or AHNT) Your **aunt** is your father's sister, your mother's sister, or your uncle's wife. *NOUN*

Bb

bank[1] (BANK) A **bank** is a place where people keep their money: My brother has a **bank** for nickels and pennies. *NOUN*

bank[2] (BANK) The **bank** of a river or lake is the ground beside it: He sat on the river **bank**. *NOUN*

bases (BAY sez)
1. A **base** is the bottom of something: The metal **bases** of the floor lamps might scratch the floor. *NOUN*

2. A **base** is also an object in some games: After hitting a home run, the player ran the **bases**. *NOUN*

basket

basket (BAS kuht)
1. A **basket** is something to carry or store things in. **Baskets** are made of straw, plastic, or strips of wood. *NOUN*

2. In basketball a **basket** is used as a goal. The **basket** is made of a metal ring with a net hanging from it. *NOUN*

bellowed (BELL ohd) To **bellow** is to make a loud, deep noise: The moose **bellowed** angrily at the man. *VERB*

birthday (BERTH day) A **birthday** is the day that a person was born or something was started: Our country's **birthday** is July 4th. *NOUN*

blame (BLAYM) To **blame** is to hold someone responsible for something bad or wrong. *VERB*

blankets (BLANG kuhts) **Blankets** are soft, warm coverings for beds: We bought new, wool **blankets**. *NOUN*

bleachers (BLEE cherz) **Bleachers** are benches for people attending games or other outdoor events. *NOUN*

block (BLOK)
1. A **block** is a thick piece of wood or plastic: My little brother held one green **block** and two blue ones. *NOUN*
2. If you **block** something, you fill it so that nothing can pass by: I saw a large truck **block** traffic. *VERB*
3. A **block** is also an area of a city that has a street on each side: I walked down the **block** to my friend's house. *NOUN*

borrow (BAR oh or BOR oh) If you **borrow** something, you get it from a person or place just for a while: I like to **borrow** books from the library. *VERB*

branches (BRANCH ez)
1. **Branches** are the part of the tree that grow out from the trunk: Swings hung from the tree's **branches**. *NOUN*
2. **Branches** are small parts of something: The **branches** of the river had quiet water. *NOUN*

brooding (BROOD ing) **Brooding** is to hang over as if to cover: The **brooding** storm clouds settled over the town. *ADJECTIVE*

building

building (BIL ding) A **building** is something that has been built. A **building** has walls and a roof. Schools, houses, and barns are **buildings**. *NOUN*

bulges (BUHL jez) **Bulges** are an outward swelling: The air in the man's jaws made **bulges** in his cheeks. *NOUN*

bumpy (BUHM pee) If something is **bumpy**, it is rough or has a lot of bumps: This street is too **bumpy** to skate on. *ADJECTIVE*

burning (BERN ing) **Burning** means to be on fire: Dad carefully watched the **burning** leaves. *ADJECTIVE*

Cc

campfire (KAMP fyr) A **campfire** is an outdoor fire used for cooking or staying warm. *NOUN*

cattle (KAT uhl) **Cattle** are animals raised for their meat, milk, or skins. Cows and bulls are **cattle**. *NOUN PLURAL*

chased (CHAYST) When you **chase** someone or something, you run after them: The children **chased** the ball down the hill. *VERB*

cheers (CHEERZ) When you **cheer**, you call out or yell loudly to show you like something: She **cheers** for her team. *VERB*

chewing

chewing (CHOO ing) When you **chew** something, you crush it with your teeth: He was **chewing** the nuts. *VERB*

chuckle (CHUK uhl) When you **chuckle**, you laugh softly: She will **chuckle** when she sees her gift. *VERB*

chuckwagon (CHUK WAG uhn) A **chuckwagon** is a wagon or truck that carries food and cooking equipment for cowhands. *NOUN*

clattering (KLAT tuhr ing) **Clattering** is having a loud, rattling noise: The **clattering** dishes woke me up. *ADJECTIVE*

climbed (KLYMD) When you **climb**, you go up something, usually by using your hands and feet: The children **climbed** into the bus. *VERB*

clubhouse (KLUB HOWSS) A **clubhouse** is a building used by a group of people joined together for some special reason. *NOUN*

clung (KLUNG)
1. If you **clung**, you held tightly to someone or something: He **clung** to his father's hand. *VERB*
2. **Clung** means to have stuck to something: The vine **clung** to the wall. *VERB*

collects (kuh LEKTS) If you **collect** things, you bring them together or gather them together: The student **collects** the crayons. *VERB*

colonies (KOL uh neez) A **colony** is a group of people who leave their own country to settle in another land but who still remain citizens of their own country: The thirteen British **colonies** became the United States of America. *NOUN*

cowboy

Congress (KONG gris) **Congress** is the national legislative body of the United States. **Congress** has two parts, the Senate and the House of Representatives. *NOUN*

cowboy (KOW boi) A **cowboy** is a person who works on a cattle ranch. **Cowboys** also take part in rodeos. *NOUN*

crawls (KRAWLZ) When you **crawl** you move on your hands and knees or with your body close to the ground: The lizard **crawls** across the floor. *VERB*

cycle (SY kuhl) A **cycle** is a series of events that repeats itself in the same order over and over again: A frog's life **cycle** begins as an egg. *NOUN*

Dd

downhearted (DOWN HART id) To be **downhearted** is to be depressed or discouraged: The team was **downhearted** because we lost the last game. *ADJECTIVE*

dripping

dripping (DRIP ing) When something **drips**, it falls in drops: The rain was **dripping** on the roof. *VERB*

drum (DRUHM) A **drum** is a musical instrument that makes a sound when it is beaten. A **drum** is hollow with a cover stretched tight over each end. *NOUN*

drum

dugout (DUHG OWT) A **dugout** is a small shelter at the side of a baseball field, used by players not on the field: The team sat in the **dugout** while the batters took turns. *NOUN*

Ee

exploring (ek SPLOR ing) When you are **exploring**, you are traveling to discover new areas: Astronauts are **exploring** outer space. *VERB*

Ff

fair¹ (FAIR) If you are **fair**, you go by the rules. People who are **fair** treat everyone the same: Try to be **fair** in everything you do. *ADJECTIVE*

fair² (FAIR) A **fair** is an outdoor show of farm animals and other things: We enjoyed ourselves at the county **fair**. *NOUN*

fair

favorite (FAY ver it)
1. Your **favorite** thing is the one you like better than all the others: What is your **favorite** color? *ADJECTIVE*

2. A **favorite** is a person or thing that you like very much: Pizza is a **favorite** with me. *NOUN*

feverishly (FEE vuhr ish lee) When something is done **feverishly**, it is done in an excited or restless way: We packed **feverishly** for the trip. *ADVERB*

field (FEE uhld) A **field** is a piece of land used for a special purpose: The football **field** needs to be mowed. *NOUN*

fierce (FEERS) When something is **fierce**, it is very great or strong: A **fierce** wind blew the tree house down. *ADJECTIVE*

fingers (FING gerz) Your **fingers** are the five end parts of your hand. *NOUN*

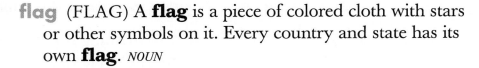

fingers

fireproof (FYR proof) A thing that is **fireproof** is almost impossible to burn: Steel and concrete are **fireproof**. *ADJECTIVE*

flag

flag (FLAG) A **flag** is a piece of colored cloth with stars or other symbols on it. Every country and state has its own **flag**. *NOUN*

flashes (FLASH ez) To **flash** is to give a light or flame: The light **flashes** on and off. *VERB*

forties (FOR teez) The **forties** are the 1940s: My granddad was born in the **forties**. *NOUN*

freedom (FREE duhm) **Freedom** is not being under someone else's control or rule. *NOUN*

fruit

fruit (FROOT) **Fruit** is the part of a tree, bush, or vine that has seeds in it and is good to eat. Apples, oranges, strawberries, and bananas are **fruit**. *NOUN*

Gg

galloped (GAL uhpt) To **gallop** is to run very fast: The horse **galloped** down the road. *VERB*

443

giant

giant (JY uhnt)
1. In stories, a **giant** is a person who is very large. *NOUN*
2. If something is **giant**, it is much bigger than usual: We made a **giant** sandwich for lunch. *ADJECTIVE*

glee (GLEE) **Glee** is a feeling of great delight or lively joy: The children at the party laughed with **glee** at the clown. *NOUN*

grabbed (GRABD) When you **grab** something, you take it suddenly: The dog **grabbed** the bone. *VERB*

greatest (GRAYT est) If something is the **greatest**, it is the best and most important: He thought it was the **greatest** book he had ever read. *ADJECTIVE*

Hh

harvest (HAR vist)
1. A **harvest** is the ripe crops that are picked after the growing season is over: The corn **harvest** was poor after the hot, dry summer. *NOUN*
2. When you **harvest**, you gather in the crops and store them: We **harvest** the apples in late fall. *VERB*

hatchet (HACH it) A **hatchet** is a small ax with a handle about a foot long, for use with one hand: Dad chopped the log with a **hatchet**. *NOUN*

herd

herd (HERD) A **herd** is a group of the same kind of animals: We saw a **herd** of cows when we drove through the country. *NOUN*

hydrant (HY druhnt) A **hydrant** is a large water pipe that sticks up out of the ground. It has places where firefighters can connect hoses. *NOUN*

Ii

ideas (eye DEE uhz) **Ideas** are thoughts or plans: The class had different **ideas** on how to spend the money. *NOUN*

important (im PORT uhnt) Something that is **important** has a lot of meaning or worth: Learning to read is **important**. *ADJECTIVE*

insect

insects (IN sekts) **Insects** are small animals with six legs and bodies that have three parts. Most **insects** have four wings. Flies, bees, butterflies, and mosquitoes are **insects**. *NOUN*

Jj

jingle (JING uhl)
1. To **jingle** is to make or cause a sound like little bells. *VERB*
2. A **jingle** is a cone-shaped piece of tin sewn in rows onto a Native American dress. *NOUN*

Ll

lightning (LYT ning) **Lightning** is a flash of electricity in the sky. The sound that **lightning** makes is thunder. *NOUN*

Louisville slugger (LOO ee vil SLUG ger) A **Louisville slugger** is one kind of a baseball bat. NOUN

Mm

moccasins

masks (MASKS) **Masks** are coverings that hide or protect your face: The firefighters wear gas **masks**. NOUN

moccasins (MOK uh suhnz) A **moccasin** is a soft leather shoe or sandal, often without an attached heel. Many Native Americans wore **moccasins**, often made of deer hide. NOUN

Nn

nicknames (NIK naymz) **Nicknames** are names used instead of real names: Ed is a **nickname** for Edward. NOUN

ninetieth (NYN tee ith) **Ninetieth** is next after the 89th: Great-grandmother celebrated her **ninetieth** birthday. ADJECTIVE

nudging (NUJ ing) **Nudging** means to give a slight push: The mother cat was **nudging** her kittens along. VERB

Oo

outrigger (OWT RIG er) An **outrigger** is a framework that sticks out from the side of a light boat, canoe, or other vehicle to keep it from turning over: The **outrigger** helped to steady the fire truck. NOUN

Pp

patchwork (PACH werk) **Patchwork** is pieces of cloth of various colors or shapes sewed together: Mother made the quilt from **patchwork**. *NOUN*

picnic (PIK nik) A **picnic** is a party with a meal outdoors: Our class had a **picnic** at the park. *NOUN*

piñata

piñata (pee NYAH tuh) A **piñata** is a decorated shape filled with candy, fruit, and small toys and hung at holiday time in Mexico and other Latin American countries. Blindfolded children swing sticks in order to break the **piñata** to get what is inside. *NOUN*

plate (PLAYT)
1. A **plate** is a dish that is almost flat and is usually round. We eat food from **plates**. *NOUN*
2. A **plate** is a hard rubber slab that a baseball player stands beside to hit the ball. *NOUN*

pond

pond (POND) A **pond** is water with land all around it. A **pond** is smaller than a lake and does not have waves. *NOUN*

pounds (POWNDZ) To **pound** is to hit something hard again and again: She **pounds** the door with her fist. *VERB*

pours (PORZ) When it **pours**, it rains a lot: The rain **pours** down on the city. *VERB*

powerful (POW er fuhl) **Powerful** is being strong and having great force: The runner had **powerful** legs. *ADJECTIVE*

practice (PRAK tiss) A **practice** is a training session: Coach says that to play the game, you must go to **practice**. *NOUN*

present¹ (PREZ uhnt) Another word for **present** is *here*. If you are **present**, you are not absent: Every member of the class is **present** today. *ADJECTIVE*

present

present² (PREZ uhnt) A **present** is a gift. A **present** is something that someone gives you or that you give someone: His uncle sent him a birthday **present**. *NOUN*

pressing (PRESS ing)
1. **Pressing** is pushing something in a steady way: The child is **pressing** the elevator button. *VERB*

2. When you **press** clothes, you make them smooth with a hot iron: I was **pressing** my shirt to get out the wrinkles. *VERB*

pretended (pri TEND ed) To **pretend** is to make believe that something is real when it is not: We **pretended** that we were camping. *VERB*

Qq

quickly (KWIK lee) **Quickly** means in a short time: When I asked him a question, he answered **quickly**. *ADVERB*

quilt (KWILT) A **quilt** is a soft covering for a bed. A **quilt** is usually made from two pieces of cloth sewn together with soft material between them. *NOUN*

quilt

Rr

railroad (RAYL rohd) A **railroad** is a road or track of two steel rails. Trains run on **railroads**. *NOUN*

regalia (ri GAY lee uh) **Regalia** are the decorations of any society: He wore the **regalia** of the Lakota Indians. *NOUN*

roar (ROR) A **roar** is a loud, deep sound: The **roar** of the lion frightened some people at the zoo. *NOUN*

rolling (ROHL ling) **Rolling** is making deep loud sounds: The **rolling** thunder woke the baby. *ADJECTIVE*

root (ROOT)
1. The **root** is the part of a plant that grows underground. A plant gets food and water through its **roots**. *NOUN*

2. A **root** is also a word from which other words are made. In the words *rounder* and *roundest*, the **root** is *round*. *NOUN*

roundup (ROWND up) A **roundup** is the act of driving or bringing cattle together from long distances. *NOUN*

Ss

sailed (SAYLD) When something **sails**, it travels on the water or through the air: The ball **sailed** out of the ballpark. *VERB*

449

scent (SENT) A **scent** is a nice smell: Helen loved the **scent** of freshly baked cookies. *NOUN*

sewer (SOO er) A **sewer** is an underground drain that carries away waste water and trash. *NOUN*

shed (SHED) To **shed** is to let hair, skin, or fur fall off: The dog **shed** on the rug. *VERB*

shuffled (SHUF uhld) To **shuffle** is to scrape or drag your feet while walking: We **shuffled** along the slippery sidewalk. *VERB*

signmaker (SYN mayk er) A **signmaker** makes marks or words on a sign that tell you what to do or not to do. *NOUN*

silver (SIL ver) **Silver** is a shiny white metal. **Silver** is used to make coins, jewelry, and other things. *NOUN*

skin (SKIN) **Skin** is the outside covering of human and animal bodies, plants, fruits, and seeds: Her **skin** was red from too much sun. *NOUN*

soar

smooth (SMOOTH) When something is **smooth**, it has an even surface. Something that is **smooth** is not bumpy or rough: The road was very **smooth**. *ADJECTIVE*

soar (SOR) To **soar** is to fly at a great height: Did you see the kite **soar** in the air? *VERB*

soil

soil¹ (SOIL) **Soil** is the top layer of the earth. **Soil** is dirt: Our garden has such rich **soil** that almost anything will grow in it. *NOUN*

soil² (SOIL) If you **soil** something, you make it dirty: The dust will **soil** her white gloves. *VERB*

spawn (SPAWN) **Spawn** is the eggs of fish, frogs, shellfish, and other animals growing or living in water. *NOUN*

special (SPESH uhl)
1. If something is **special**, it is unusual or different in some way: Your birthday is a **special** day. *ADJECTIVE*

2. A **special** is a TV show produced for one showing: I saw a TV **special** on wolves. *NOUN*

spectators (SPEK tay ters) A **spectator** is someone who looks on without taking part. There were many **spectators** at the ball game. *NOUN*

stars (STARZ)
1. **Stars** are the very bright points of light that shine in the sky at night: On a clear night, the **stars** are very bright. *NOUN*

2. **Stars** are also shapes that have five or six points: I drew **stars** on the paper. *NOUN*

station (STAY shuhn) A **station** is a building or place used for a special reason: The man went to the police **station**. *NOUN*

stitched (STICHT) To **stitch** is to sew or fasten something with **stitches**: Mom **stitched** the hole in my sweater. *VERB*

storm

storm (STORM) A **storm** is a strong wind with rain, snow, or hail. Some **storms** have lightning and thunder. *NOUN*

stray (STRAY) A **stray** is a lost animal: That cat is a **stray** that we took in. *NOUN*

stripes (STRYPS) **Stripes** are long, narrow bands of color: Our flag has seven red **stripes** and six white **stripes**. *NOUN*

strong (STRAWNG) Something that is **strong** has power. A **strong** person can lift and carry things that are heavy. **Strong** means not weak: A **strong** wind blew down the tree. *ADJECTIVE*

stuffing (STUF ing) **Stuffing** is material used to fill or pack something: The **stuffing** is coming out of the pillow. *NOUN*

Tt

tantrum (TAN truhm) A **tantrum** is a sudden, childish outburst of bad temper or ill humor: The girl had a **tantrum** when she couldn't get her way. *NOUN*

tears (TEERZ) **Tears** are drops of salty water that come from your eye. **Tears** fall when you cry. *NOUN*

tendrils

tendrils (TEN druhls) A **tendril** is the thin, curling part of a climbing plant that attaches itself to something and helps support the plant: The ivy plant sent out long, thin **tendrils**. *NOUN*

threw (THROO) When you **threw** something, you sent it through the air: She **threw** the ball back to him. *VERB*

thunder (THUHN der) **Thunder** is the loud noise from the sky that comes after a flash of lightning. *NOUN*

tía (TEE uh) **Tía** is the Spanish word for aunt: My **tía** is my mother's sister. *NOUN*

tightly (TYT lee) When something is tied **tightly**, it is firmly tied: The rope was tied **tightly**. *ADVERB*

townspeople (TOWNZ pee puhl) **Townspeople** are the men, women, and children who live in a village or town: The **townspeople** enjoyed the fair. *NOUN*

trails (TRAYLZ) **Trails** are paths across fields or through the woods: Two **trails** led to the river. *NOUN*

treat (TREET) A **treat** is a gift of food, drink, a free ticket, or the like: She gave us **treats** on the last day of school. *NOUN*

453

trouble (TRUHB uhl)

1. **Trouble** is something that makes you upset, bothers you, or gives you pain: I had a lot of **trouble** working those math problems. *NOUN*

2. If you are in **trouble**, people are angry or upset with you: You will be in **trouble** if you knock that can of paint over. *NOUN*

truest (TROO ist) To be **true** is to be faithful and loyal: She is the **truest** friend I have. *ADJECTIVE*

trunks (TRUHNGKS) **Trunks** are large boxes for carrying clothes. *NOUN*

trunks

Uu

unpacked (uhn PAKT) To **unpack** is to take things out that were packed in a box, trunk, or other container: He **unpacked** his clothes. *VERB*

usually (YOO zhoo uhl lee) **Usually** tells how something is seen, found, or happening most of the time: We **usually** eat at six o'clock. *ADVERB*

Vv

vegetarians (vej uh TAIR ee uhns) A **vegetarian** is someone who eats vegetables but no meat: **Vegetarians** like to eat fruit. *NOUN*

vine (VYN) A **vine** is a plant that grows along the ground. Some **vines** climb up walls and fences. Pumpkins, melons, and grapes grow on **vines**. *NOUN*

voice (VOISS) Your **voice** is the sound you make with your mouth. You use your **voice** when you speak, sing, or shout. *NOUN*

Ww

wagged (WAGD) To **wag** is to move from side to side or up and down: The dog **wagged** her tail. *VERB*

wisdom (WIZ duhm) **Wisdom** is knowledge and good judgment based on experience: The leader's **wisdom** guided the group through the woods. *NOUN*

wither (WITH er) To **wither** is to make or become dry and lifeless; dry up: The hot sun will **wither** the plants. *VERB*

wondered (WUHN derd) When you **wondered** about something, you wanted to know about it: He **wondered** what time it was. *VERB*

wonderful (WUHN der fuhl) If something is **wonderful**, you like it very much: The ocean was a **wonderful** sight. *ADJECTIVE*

wrapped

wrapped (RAPT) When you **wrap** something, you cover it up, usually with paper: We **wrapped** presents all morning. *VERB*

Unit 4

The Quilt Story

English	Spanish
blankets	mantas
pretended	imaginó
quilt	edredón
stuffing	relleno
trunks	baúles
unpacked	desempacaron
wrapped	envolvió

Life Cycle of a Pumpkin

English	Spanish
bumpy	desiguales
fruit	fruta
harvest	cosecha
roots	raíz
smooth	lisas
soil	tierra
vine	enredadera

Frogs

English	Spanish
crawls	gatea
insects	insectos
pond	estanque
powerful	fuertes
shed	mudado
skin	piel
wonderful	maravilloso

I Like Where I Am

English	Spanish
block	cuadra
chuckle	echan risitas
fair	justo
giant	enorme
strong	fuertes
tears	lágrimas
trouble	problemas

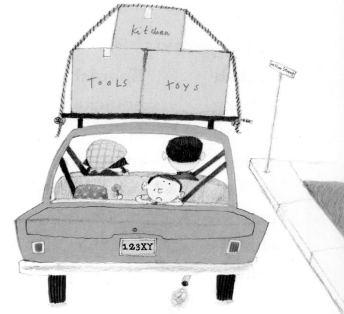

Helen Keller and the Big Storm

English	Spanish
angry	enojada
branches	ramas
clung	se aferró
fingers	dedos
picnic	comida campestre
pressing	presionando
special	especial

457

Unit 5

Firefighter!

English	Spanish
building	edificio
burning	ardiente
masks	máscaras
quickly	rápidamente
roar	rugido
station	estación
tightly	bien

One Dark Night

English	Spanish
lightning	relámpago
flashes	destella
pounds	golpea
pours	llueve a cántaros
rolling	retumbando
storm	tormenta
thunder	truenos

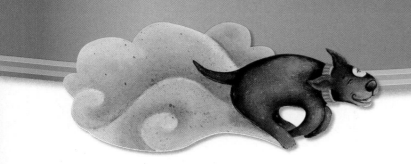

Bad Dog, Dodger!

English	Spanish
chased	persiguieron
chewing	mordiendo
dripping	goteando
grabbed	agarró
practice	entrenamiento
treat	galletas (de perro)
wagged	meneó

The Signmaker's Assistant

English	Spanish
afternoon	tarde
blame	culpen
ideas	idea
important	importante
signmaker	rotulista
townspeople	ciudadanos

Horace and Morris but mostly Dolores

English	Spanish
adventure	aventura
climbed	subieron
clubhouse	casa del club
exploring	explorando
greatest	mejores
truest	más verdaderos
wondered	se preguntaba

Unit 6

Just Like Josh Gibson

English	Spanish
bases	bases
cheers	gritos de entusiasmo
field	campo
plate	base meta
sailed	volaban
threw	tiró

Red, White, and Blue: The Story of the American Flag

English	Spanish
	Estados Unidos
	cumpleaños
	bandera
	libertad
	apodos
	estrellas
	franjas

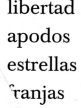

459

A Birthday Basket for Tía

English	Spanish
aunt	tía
bank	alcancía
basket	cesta
collects	recoge
favorite	favorito
present	regalo

Cowboys

English	Spanish
campfire	fuego (de campamento)
cattle	ganado
cowboy	vaquero
galloped	galoparon
herd	manada
railroad	ferrocarril
trails	sendas

Jingle Dancer

English	Spanish
borrow	pedir prestado
clattering	ruidosos
drum	tambor
jingle	cascabeles
silver	plata
voice	voz

461

Acknowledgments

Text

Page 16: *The Quilt Story* by Tony Johnston and illustrated by Tomie dePaola. Text Copyright © Tony Johnston, 1985. Illustrations Copyright © Tomie dePaola, 1985. Published by arrangement with G.P. Putnam's Sons, a division of Penguin Young Readers Group, a member of Penguin Group (USA) Inc. All rights reserved.

Page 46: *The Life Cycle of a Pumpkin* by Ron Fridell and Patricia Walsh. Harcourt Global Library, art of Harcourt Education Ltd. Reprinted by permission.

Page 62: From *Where Fish Go in Winter And Other Great Mysteries* by Amy Goldman Koss, copyright © 1987 by Amy Goldman Koss, text. Used by permission of Dial Books for Young Readers, A Division of Penguin Young Readers Group, A Member of Penguin Group (USA) Inc., 345 Hudson Street, New York, NY 10014. All rights reserved.

Page 70: From *Frogs* by Gail Gibbons. Copyright © 1993 by Gail Gibbons. All rights reserved. Reprinted from *Frogs* by permission of Holiday House, Inc.

Page 90: From *Life Cycles* by Michael Elsohn Ross; illustrated by Gustav Moore. Text copyright © 2001 by Michael Elsohn Ross; illustrations copyright © 2001 by Gustav Moore. Used by permission of Millbrook Press, a division of Lerner Publishing Group. All rights reserved.

Page 100: *I Like Where I Am* by Jessica Harper and illustrated by Brian Karas. Text Copyright © Jessica Harper 2004. Illustrations Copyright © Brian Karas, 2004 Published by arrangement with G.P. Putnam's Sons, a division of Penguin Young Readers Group, a member of Penguin Group (USA) Inc. All rights reserved.

Page 128: Reprinted with the permission of Aladdin Paperbacks, an imprint of Simon & Schuster Children's Publishing Division from *Helen Keller and the Big Storm* by Patricia Lakin. Copyright © 2002 Patricia Lakin.

Page 144: Reprinted with the permission of Aladdin Paperbacks, an imprint of Simon & Schuster Children's Publishing Division from *Wind* by Marion Dane Bauer. Copyright © 2003 Marion Dane Bauer.

Page 158: *Fire Fighter!* by Angela Royston. Copyright © 1998 Dorling Kindersley Limited, London. Reprinted by permission.

Page 184: *One Dark Night* written by Hazel Hutchins and illustrations by Susan Hartung. Text copyright © 2001 by Hazel Hutchins. Illustrations copyright © 2001 by Susan Hartung. Published by arrangement with Viking Children's Books, a division of Penguin Young Readers Group, a member of Penguin Group (USA) Inc.

Page 204: Isabel Joshlin Glaser for "Adoption". Reprinted from *You and Me* by Salley Mavor, 1997. Reprinted by permission of Isabel Joshlin Glaser.

Page 205: *"The Stray Cat"* by Eve Merriam. Used by permission of Marian Reiner.

Page 212: Reprinted with the permission of Margaret K. McElderry Books, an imprint of Simon & Schuster Children's Publishing Division from *Bad Dog, Dodger!* by Barbara Abercrombie. Text copyright © 2002 Barbara Abercrombie.

Page 238: From *Horace and Morris but Mostly Dolores.* Text copyright © 1999 by James Howe. Illustrations copyright © 1999 by Amy Walrod. Reprinted with permission of Atheneum Books for Young Readers, Simon & Schuster Children's Publishing Division. All rights reserved.

Page 268: *The Signmaker's Assistant* by Tedd Arnold. Copyright © 1992 by Tedd Arnold. Published by arrangement with Dial Books for Young Readers, a division of Penguin Young Readers Group, a member of Penguin Group (USA) Inc..

Page 286: Action Without Borders Web site, www.idealist.org/kt/youthorgs.html. Reprinted by permission.

Page 300: From *Just Like Josh Gibson.* Text copyright © 2004 by Angela Johnson. Illustrations copyright © 2004 by Beth Peck. Reprinted with permission of Simon & Schuster Books for Young Readers, Simon & Schuster Children's Publishing Division. All rights reserved.

Page 326: *Red, White, And Blue* by John Herman, and illustrated by Robin Roraback. Text Copyright © John Herman, 1998. Illustration Copyright © Robin Roraback, 1998. Published by arrangement with Grosset & Dunlap, a division of Penguin Young Readers Group, a member of Penguin Group (USA) Inc. All rights reserved.

Page 354: From *A Birthday Basket for Tía.* Text copyright © 1992 by Pat Mora. Illustrations copyright © 1992 by Cecily Lang. Reprinted with permission of Simon & Schuster Books for Young Readers, Simon & Schuster Children's Publishing Division. All rights reserved.

Page 370: From www.kidparties.com/traditions.htm. Reprinted by permission.

Page 380: *Cowboys* by Lucille Recht Penner, illustrated by Ben Carter, Grosset & Dunlap, 1996.

Page 404: From *The Cowboy's Handbook* by Tod Cody, copyright © 1996 by Breslich & Foss, entire text and compilation of illustrations. Used by permission of Cobblehill Books, an affiliate of Dutton Children's Books, A Division of Penguin Young Readers Group, A Member of Penguin Group (USA) Inc., 345 Hudson Street, New York, NY 10014. All rights reserved.

Page 412: *Jingle Dancer* by Cynthia Leitich Smith, illustrated by Cornelius Van Wright and Ying-Hwa Hu. Text copyright © 2000 by Cynthia Leitich Smith. Illustrations copyright © 2000 by Cornelius Van Wright and Ying-Hwa Hu.

Page 428: From "Celebrating the Buffalo Days" from *Buffalo Days* by Diane Hoyt-Goldsmith, Photographs by Lawrence Migdale, Illustrations by Ted Furlo. Text copyright © 1997 by Diane Hoyt-Goldsmith. Photographs copyright © 1997 by Lawrence Migdale. All rights reserved. Reprinted from *Buffalo Days* by permission of Holiday House, Inc.

Illustrations

10 MAN ON THE MOON (A DAY IN THE LIFE OF BOB). Copyright © 2002 Simon Bartram. First published in Great Britain by Templar Publishing. Reproduced by permission of the publisher/Candlewick Press, Inc., Cambridge, MA.
89, 117, 129, 150–151, 174–177, 212–225, 250, 292–293, 345, 403, 434–435 Laura Ovresat
128–140 Troy Howell
204 Jui Ishida
316–319 Clint Hansen
326–336, 340–342 Shannan Stirnweiss
338, 400–401 Derek Grinnell
354–367 Cecily Lang

Photographs

Every effort has been made to secure permission and provide appropriate credit for photographic material. The publisher deeply regrets any omission and pledges to correct errors called to its attention in subsequent editions.

Unless otherwise acknowledged, all photographs are the property of Scott Foresman, a division of Pearson Education.

Photo locators denoted as follows: Top (T), Center (C), Bottom (B), Left (L), Right (R), Background (Bkgd).

13 Corbis
15 © Michael Boys/Corbis
35 (CR, BR) Getty Images, (TR) © Cape Cod Travel
36 © Cape Cod Travel
37 © Lee Snider/Corbis
38 © Amy Dykens/Cape Cod Travel
39 © Cape Cod Travel
43 © Renee Lynn/Corbis
45 (TR, BR) Getty Images
46 (Bkgd) Getty Images, (TR) © Royalty-Free/Corbis
48 (CR) © Royalty-Free/Corbis, (TC) © Ben Klaffe
49 (TL) Getty Images, (TR) © Dwight R. Kuhn
50 (TL, TR) © Dwight R. Kuhn
51 (TC) © Shmuel Thaler/Index Stock Imagery, (CR) © Dwight R. Kuhn
52 (T) © Steve Solum/Index Stock Imagery, (CR) © Ben Klaffe
53 (T, TR) © Dwight R. Kuhn
54 (T, BR) © Ben Klaffe
55 (T) © Reuters/Corbis, (CR) © Dwight R. Kuhn
56 (T) © Dwight R. Kuhn, (CR) Getty Images
57 (T) © Barry Lewis/Corbis, (CR) © Matthew Klein/Corbis
58 (TL) © Tony Freeman/PhotoEdit, (TR) © Royalty-Free/Corbis
59 © Richard Hamilton Smith/Corbis
60 © Dwight R. Kuhn
61 (BL) © Dwight R. Kuhn, (BR) © Ben Klaffe, (TL) © Matthew Klein/Corbis, (TC) © Royalty-Free/Corbis, (BC) Getty Images, (CL) © Alex Cohn
63 © David Aubrey/Corbis
65 © Royalty-Free/Corbis
67 (BL) © Royalty-Free/Corbis, (BC) © Richard Cummins/Corbis
68–69 Getty Images

Glossary

The contents of this glossary have been adapted from *My First Dictionary.* Copyright © 2000, Pearson Education, Inc.